# ENJOY

# LIFE

*THE INTENTIONAL LIVING GUIDE FOR*

*BUILDING A BEAUTIFUL LIFE AND BUSINESS*

---

# STACIA

# PIERCE

*Enjoy Life*
*Second Edition*

ISBN 978-0-9977656-7-0

Published by Ultimate Lifestyle Enterprises, LLC
4630 S. Kirkman Road #343
Orlando, FL 32811

Printed in the United States of America.

**Author's Autograph Page**

*This Book Belongs to:*

_____

**Stacia Pierce**

3

Enjoy Life


**Other Books by Stacia Pierce:**


Stacia: My Life in Style (eBook)

Inspired to Succeed (eBook)

Success Attraction Notes & Quotes

# ENJOY LIFE

## Table of Contents

# External *Clues*

# Personal *Muse*

# Acknowledgements

I am blessed to be surrounded by numerous people who support and believe in me each day.

A Colorful Thanks to:
The thousands of women who support my efforts, my Dream Life Center family and my coaching clients. You motivate me to keep creating ways to improve lives.

My wonderful children Ariana and Ryan who bring me joy daily.

My husband James who inspires me each day to do the impossible. Your love and encouragement are priceless. Thank you for making my life more enjoyable than I ever imagined.

# Introduction

*a* life well lived is not one in which you merely exist. It is a life of balance, joy and overall well-being. With dogged tenacity, we race through our day, many times without a clue as to why we are placed on this earth. Enjoy life. How does one accomplish such a state of living? Create it. Enjoying life is a skill that you can develop. This book is set up to help you improve your "living skills." I've written *Enjoy Life* to give you step-by-step instructions to extract the drudgery from your existence and add a little "play" to your day. When genuine pleasure is a part of your daily routine, you'll find that life becomes more meaningful and balanced.

To deny yourself consistently of doing those things that bring you joy is self destructive and will eventually lead to resentment. Our personalities, preferences and problem solving abilities are woven together for purpose. Everything about your character is a hint to your God-given assignment. Enjoying life is not frivolous. There is a definite thread between what you enjoy simply for pleasure and what you are called to do for life. Through this book, you will get in touch with activities that bring you authentic delight, thus leading you to a more fulfilling existence.

At the end of each chapter I have included the *"Create a Collage"* pages to provide you with an inspirational, fun way to immediately put your learning into practice. In my personal life I create vision boards that I keep in front of me in my personal space at home, and collages in my journals of words and pictures of those things that I desire to see happen in my home, life and businesses. This visual aid is what helps keep me fueled by a burning desire to see my goals and dreams accomplished, and I want to share this powerful tool of manifestation with you. Here are some basic instructions to help you along, so that you too can live a more fulfilling and purposeful life.

**INSTRUCTIONS FOR CREATING YOUR COLLAGE PAGE:**

At the end of each chapter you can create your own collage of what inspires you from that subject. To bring your visual to life you must do a few things:

1) Gather some magazines, scissors, a glue stick and even bring your computer into the mix. With these tools you'll be able to pull pictures and words that go along with the particular chapter you just got through reading. If you can't find them in a magazine, search on the Internet for your favorite images and words and print them out.

2) Next, use the scissors to cut out the images and words and arrange them on the collage space. (Tip: the pages are small, so keep that in mind when gathering your images. You don't want a whole bunch of paper sticking out of the side of your book where they can get crushed.) Put your word title that coincides with the chapter at the top of your page and everything else underneath. This gives you a more focused visual of what you are believing to become real in your life.

3) Once you have a good layout, grab your glue stick and seal your vision down onto your collage space. If you're like me, this is the most exciting part, because now you have a full picture to focus on and enjoy until the real thing comes around.

4) Perfection is not the key here. These collage pages are just an extension of dreams, goals and desires to make your life more complete and enjoyable. Sometimes plans and circumstances change and you may have to rearrange some things, but that is OK. Keep visualizing and meditating on your creations and get excited about a new you.

Remember, think of this collage space as a space to fill in with all of your thoughts and feelings that convey how you want to enjoy life for that particular chapter. As you go through the chapters you will discover a recurring thread of all of your likes, desires and dreams. The collages you create will become a real-time document of you and where you will and can be to enjoy life.

Also, I've created an Enjoy Life resources page for you that can be found on my website www.LifeCoach2Women.com. It lists all of the resources, phone numbers and websites to put the power to take action right at your fingertips. Life as you know it, is over. Today is a new beginning. The contents of this book will leave you unequivocally changed and forever impacted. As of this day, you can learn to enjoy the journey and become masterfully skilled at living a wonderful life.

# Internal
## Cues

# CHAPTER 1

# Enjoy

## Living Your Best Life

*"Life does not consist of what a person possesses,
but in what possesses him"*
*– Author unknown*

I love my life! Every woman should be able to get up each day and say that from the heart. So how do you advance from the life you live now to genuinely enjoying each day? Let your imagination lead the way.

If life were a party, what kind of people would you invite? How would you decorate? What would your invitations look like? What kind of games would you play? Well, *your* life is a party. You have been blessed with the gift of life and the life you live should be a grand celebration. *Living your best life requires that you host this grand celebration.* I am here to assist you in your party planning. Throughout this book I will help you choose your paper, decorate, and entertain. As a business and lifestyle coach, I've recognized that having the proper tools is important to getting things done, and getting them done right. So throughout this lifestyle guide, I will give you the resources and principles you must know to host your own celebration and live your best life.

Life is so precious that we should be very careful not to waste a minute of it. To live your best life your planning must begin today. There are many different ingredients that you must blend together to create an enjoyable life. Who you are and how you operate should be anchored on your purpose in life. Your unique assignment should direct you on your daily path.

Everything I do is to help other women and entrepreneurs Enjoy Life. That is the sum total of why I was put on this Earth. I am called to motivate women and business owners to teach them how to reach their greatest potential in business and life. Even the fun things that I enjoy are closely related to my purpose. What are you called to do?

How to reach your best life becomes clear once you learn to examine your inner thoughts and impressions and turn them into your outward activities and expressions. To do this you must learn balance. Each of our lives are filled with internal cues and external clues. In living my best life, I have discovered how to balance the two and I'll show you how to do the same.

**External clues** are hints from your surroundings that lead you toward purpose. They are things that you are drawn to like certain colors, styles, or activities that you enjoy. My signature colors are fuchsia, yellow, orange and green. I love to splash these vibrant hues anywhere I can to brighten up the atmosphere.

I favor very modern styles in art, furniture, and architecture. When I evaluate the external things that I enjoy, it denotes my personal style of coaching. With every event I host, I want to brighten people's lives and add giant splashes of color. With every product, seminar, and book, I try to present timeless principles of success in a very new and modern way. My external clues always provide inspiration and little suggestions to keep me focused on my purpose.

**Internal cues** are directives that come from the inner most part of you. They provide suggestions and hints as to what you're called to do. It's that still, small voice that whispers a life changing thought.

**Living your best life is also about being creative.** It's a new approach to living that challenges you to deal with problems and take opportunities in a fresh new way. There are a few rules that I live by that serve as a guide for me to enjoy life. Each rule is important to the overall balance of your life. There may not be a specific chapter on each one of these things, but their topical presence throughout the text is made known nonetheless. It would require volumes of writings to fully describe each of my Enjoy Life rules, but I will make an honorable attempt to briefly explain the essence of each one. The chapters that follow will provide the delicious details.

**Live Artfully.** Appreciate skillfully crafted masterpieces created by artists that have dedicated their lives to presenting the world with objects of beauty. Don't travel on your life's journey without appreciating art. Take time out to visit museums and galleries. Become a collector. When you can, purchase a unique art piece that you love looking at. After you do this several times, you'll have started your art collection.

**Live Beautifully.** Take every opportunity to absorb the beauty that surrounds you. Take the time to add beauty to your life through flowers, decorating, shopping, pampering yourself, and much more.

**Dare to Live Playfully.** You can do this by enjoying your leisure time and engaging in activities which are socially exciting and that fit your personal style. You will find external clues to your destiny by planning girlfriend adventures, enjoying your Saturday mornings, entertaining and dining out.

**Live Resourcefully.** Have an "I can do it" attitude. Make the most of every day. Enjoy learning, traveling, hunting and gathering. As you do, you will develop a keen sense of know-how that will lead you to becoming your personal best.

**Live Prayerfully.** I will show you how to take time out, keep your Success Journal, and write your way to the top. A spiritual balance is essential for every person's happiness.

**Live Passionately.** Get passionate about something in life. If nothing else, have a passion for living. I have a passion for coaching entrepreneurs and seeing women's lives changed. I love to see them learn and grow in order to fulfill their purpose. That passion gives me the energy to research others in business and strategies for succeeding. Then, using that knowledge and sharing principles and tools to help entrepreneurs to grow in their businesses.

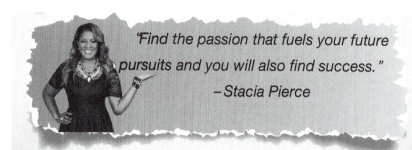

*"Find the passion that fuels your future pursuits and you will also find success."*

*– Stacia Pierce*

**What is your driving passion?** Stir it up and allow yourself to fall in love with something. Whatever pursuit stirs your passion, you will do exceedingly well. When women contact me and say they seem unable to locate their passions, I advise them to investigate. That's what prompted me to create an entire course called The Path to Purpose. You have to look around your life and search for external clues. What do you really enjoy doing? Many times the clues go unnoticed because they are such a normal part of your life. Grab your journal and write down every activity that you immensely enjoy. Review the list. As you search, you will find the passion to fuel your future pursuits.

**Live a Meaningful Life.** You will enjoy living a life of meaning and be able to take heed to the external clues and internal cues that come to light as you continue to read through the chapters. Why live a life you don't enjoy? Why not celebrate the gifts and talents that you have been given? You can and you will if you apply the principles I've outlined for you.

**Live Purposefully.** We all have a reason for being on this planet. Each of us has a special assignment. As you go through life, sharpen your sensitivity to purpose. Set appointments with yourself to visualize often. Sit and ponder your future, your plans, and your goals. As humans, we process our thoughts through visualization. Our mind sees and understands pictures very easily.

**The Millionaire's Dream Book**

I encourage each one of you to use The Millionaire's Dream Book as a companion tool when reading this book. My Dream Book is an outstanding tool I developed several years ago. It's a complete vision book that allows you to create an actual picture of the life you've always dreamed of. It adds focus to your faith and starts the process of extraordinary achievement.

Within the sections are topics that cover every area of your life and business. The Dream Book is used to create a visual of what you were called to do. Like a billboard on the side of the road, these pages will give you a vision for your life's coming attractions and steer you towards dream fulfillment.

As you read the information in this book and do the corresponding activities in *The Millionaire's Dream Book*, you will also discover exactly what it takes for you to enjoy your life. When you see where you are headed, your behavior is orchestrated accordingly. This book was created to help you enjoy living your best life by giving you a step-by-step plan on how to live a life full of meaning and discover the joy of doing so. You truly enjoy life when your personality completely serves the purpose that God has given you. My *Enjoy Life Guide* will show you how to bring these two things together.

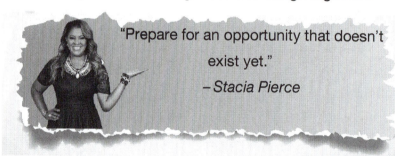

"Prepare for an opportunity that doesn't exist yet."

*– Stacia Pierce*

Living your best life is all about your purpose. It's about creating the balance. As you continue to absorb the information within these pages, look out for those external clues, a-ha moments and ideas that will be sparked along the way. Keep those pages turning and prepare for an opportunity that doesn't exist yet. **Remember, your life is a party, so let the celebration begin!**

# CREATE A COLLAGE

## Designing My Life to Enjoy:

### Living My Best Life

**Use the layout on the following page to design your vision in this area. Get glue sticks, magazines and cut out words and pictures to create an Enjoy Life Collage.**

What does your best life look like? Imagine the possibilities. Where would you work? Who would you know? What things would you do to fulfill your purpose? Create a collage that illustrates the best life style that you can imagine.

Designing a Life to Enjoy

# CREATE A COLLAGE
LifeCoach2Women.com

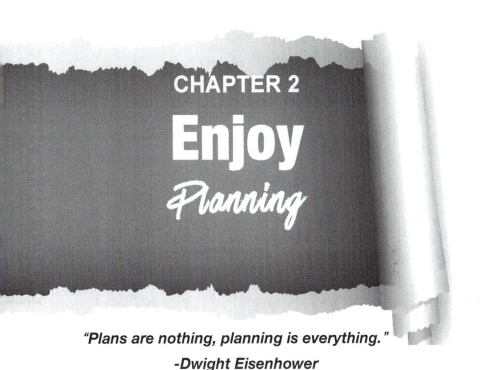

# CHAPTER 2
# Enjoy
## *Planning*

*"Plans are nothing, planning is everything."*

*-Dwight Eisenhower*

As I organized my thoughts about this chapter I continued to ask myself how do I enjoy life so much? What are the ingredients that blend and mix together to make my life exciting, worthwhile, and purposeful? One of them I noted is that I plan my life on purpose. To the best of my ability I live intentionally and purposefully. A more enjoyable state of living is discovered when you choose to live your life with purpose as your driving force.

Discovering the master plan for your life may not be as mysterious as you think. Your plans are revealed from

29

people who cross your path, places that you travel to, books you read, and audios that you listen to. That's why it's essential that you don't make decisions based on cost, but on the value that the purchase will provide.

Choosing not to plan for your purpose results in a misguided lifestyle full of potholes and wrong turns that could have been avoided. You don't have to be an ill-fated traveler; you can have the best. Your life should be fulfilling, satisfying and cause you to wake with eagerness each day. If your life doesn't quite fit that description, be aware that "happily ever after" doesn't just happen, a good life is woven with care. An enjoyable life is planned. You must pay attention to the details of life while in energetic pursuit of your inspired life plan. When you approach life with a lack of diligence, poverty and misfortune are inevitable. I believe preparation and a focused diligence to the details of my family and life have been the key to my success. The following guide is a pathfinder of sorts of my secrets and strategies that I have used in my own life and in the lives of those I have coached into discovering their purpose and managing their life with direction.

# Your Guide to Planning

## 1. Ask Questions

**You** need wisdom to plan your life and make the right decisions. Benjamin Franklin said' *"The doors of wisdom are never shut."* Wisdom is always available when we need it.

When you have to make important decisions it is imperative that you ask the right questions. If you don't know what to do next with your life, ask questions and begin to explore. With time, things will begin to be revealed to you. Pay attention and allow yourself time with uncertainty, exploring possibilities. Many times, I ask God questions at night and by the morning I have received the answer in a dream or the answer resonates within me. Even if your answer doesn't come over night, be patient; the right answer is worth the wait.

Illumination often occurs when you are doing something unrelated to the issue at hand. It can happen while showering, driving, listening to music, or being involved in another type of activity. So stay alert and keep your ears perked, eye-opening illumination may be closer than it appears.

## 2. Live by Lists

It's important to write down your lists for all different areas of your life. When it comes to planning, a list will help get all of those thoughts and ideas swirling around in your head onto paper. The great thing about making lists is that they can be brief and done quickly. It helps when you don't want to forget anything, like a grocery item or also if you're going to have a meeting and you have some last minute topics to discuss that weren't in your original notes to talk about.

I am convinced that my pen and paper empower me to progress and can do the same for you. Your lists will prevent you from forgetting life's important things. They will stimulate more progress by helping you to keep a clear vision. They will create an easy way to organize yourself and get more of the right things done, and help you be more effective in coordinating daily activities.

**Take Action**

I challenge you to start creating lists today. Choose two or three lists from the 'starter lists' below and write down at least ten items for each one. Create a to-do list for tomorrow, and make a commitment to yourself and your future success to write that daily to-do list each night for the next week.

## Starter Lists for Life

1. Your goals for the next 30 days
2. Your goals for the next year
3. Your 5-year goals
4. Tools you need to obtain to be more effective
5. Your dream vacation spots
6. People you want to meet
7. 25 things you can do to make more money

Use lists as a method to conquer your big picture vision little by little.

## 3. Create a Success Hour of Power

I am often asked how do I make the magic happen in my business and life. Certainly, I am no magician, I just wholeheartedly believe in using proven systems to get things done.

With life in general, there are a lot of roles we play and if you're not careful you can get so caught up working and giving of yourself to others around you, that you leave no time for self- rejuvenation.

This means you're stuck in the day-to-day flow, leaving no room for creativity and empowerment that you need to actually build a great life. The secret to my success can be summed up into what I call my Success Hour. It's made up of 4 daily actions in 15 minute intervals. It includes the most important activity that helps me to be in top shape to win in life.

Let's break it down:

## 15 Minutes of Prayer and Meditation

The most important part of my day is the morning hours. I awake early to pray over my life and business and meditate on my vision and plans. I usually do this in my adjoining office. Meditation keeps me centered and calm. I focus on my breathing, taking slow deep breaths until I clear my mind.

Once my mind is clear I turn my thoughts to my daily goals. I think about my day and my big picture, allowing new ideas and inclinations to flow freely so that I am aware and acknowledging the thoughts. This activity increases my creativity and helps me to develop a master plan to get more done in a day. I find it useful to think about everything I want to get done, create a prioritized list and make adjustments in this quiet moment before I actually start my day.

Insight comes early; if you sit quietly in the morning and meditate and then listen within, you will discover brilliant ideas are ready to burst out of you. You have to find your very own sweet spot where you can get quiet, relax and think big thoughts. Allow your mind to expand and see yourself productive, profitable and progressing toward your goals. This is one of the main techniques I teach to my clients because meditation helps you to transform your thinking and improve your life overall...when you are meditating on the right things!

During this time I usually am focusing on my Goal Cards and saying my affirmations as well. I use my goal cards to focus on one goal until it is accomplished. With the cards, you can write your objective, add a representative photo and write positive affirmations so that you have a good visual to meditate on. It's even smaller than a vision board so you can carry it around with you to meditate on throughout your day. In my life I've seen dramatic results from using my goal cards. So have my clients. For instance, a client set a goal to own her own barbershop and used a goal card to meditate on this goal everyday. She's now the proud owner of her own shop, debt-free. The previous owner just gave it to her free and clear. That's the power of meditation and focusing on a goal until you get results!

At the end of meditation, I usually go right into my next phase:

## 15 Minutes of Journaling

I like to write while my ideas and thoughts are fresh, so that I capture them as complete and thorough as possible. Usually when I start writing, more insight comes and I am able to add to the original thought right away.

I usually journal twice a day; in the morning and in the evening. Using The Success Journal, I plan my future and write out my dreams and goals. The journal has 5 weekly sections so that you can focus your journaling efforts on a weekly basis.

I use my journal to write a lot of action plans. I make a list of the most important things that have to be done and who needs to do it. I also create a list of talking points for my meetings as well. I also write about what I want to see and acknowledge throughout my day. I make a quick list of these things so that I stay in a place of awareness.

The Success Journal is unique because it is filled with guided prompts to steer you in the right direction with journaling. With so many areas to cover, journaling time can be fun and exciting to complete. At night, I take time to complete sections like my "I am statements" or fill in my inspiring quotes for the week so that I have them to meditate on. I always end each day completing the gratitude section. It reminds me to always stay grateful for what I have and already accomplished in my life. The more grateful you are, the more you'll find things to be grateful for.

What gets me in the mood for journaling is having all the right accessories in place. For example, I keep my favorite pens (I LOVE  Poppin' Pens) right next to my journal on my night stand. It makes it easy for me to write, morning and night.

I also keep books on my nightstand, which leads me to my next phase:

# 15 Minutes of Reading

Information changes the seasons of your life. Everyday I dedicate a minimum of 15 minutes to reading. I love reading. Every time I have taken a major shift in my business and life, I was empowered through reading. When I was transitioning my business, I was inspired to contact the author of a book I was reading. I dialed the number printed in the book and was able to reach them easily. We had an instant connection! After a few conversations I discovered that they had all the answers to my burning questions for the next phase of my business. Another time, I was looking for a way to raise enough capital to launch a new business. While at the bookstore, I started reading a book that sparked the perfect idea that empowered me to raise $10,000 in just one week.

Ideas, information and inspiration can always be found in a book. That's why I keep a stack of them on my nightstand. I am constantly consuming information and implementing what I learn. It is my biggest secret to success.

# 15 Minutes of Exercise

When you're building a business, it's easy to make excuses for not working out. However, I've learned to overcome the excuses by adding movement into my daily routine. With just 15 minutes of exercise, I have become consistent with my physical activity and healthier. I go for a "thought walk" where I actually walk and meditate simultaneously. It actually happens organically because exercising gets the blood flowing and the mind racing with new ideas. I come up with the best things while working out! Usually when I return from the walk, I write down my thoughts quickly to capture them.

When I travel, I have an in-room routine that my former trainer taught me. I sprint in place as fast as I can in 1-minute intervals. This gets the heart pumping and helps me to tone and strengthen my body while also relieving stress.

The success hour, doesn't have to happen all at once, it just needs to happen in the same day. While some activities usually flow right into the next, I often accomplish about half of the success hour in the morning and the other half at night.

Since I have implemented the success hour of power into my life, I have actually felt more freedom to do what's best for me. I don't have to be so rigid that the tasks seem like a burden. By allowing myself to get things done in 15-minute intervals throughout the day, I welcome each phase with joy and acceptance. I embrace the success habits and actually look forward to them (because I LOVE the results that I'm getting).

I challenge you to implement the Success Hour into your daily routine for a week. You'll be more confident and empowered to take on whatever is on your path to success. Be excited about your future, by implementing the Success Hour you too will experience more productivity, freedom, and joy.

## 2. Commit to a Good Mentor

What's better than walking down the road with a map? Walking down the road with a map and someone who has traveled that road before. That's where mentorship comes in. A good mentor or coach will help you navigate towards purpose. He or she will make demands on your skills and abilities, and cause you to grow and see things in a new way. Look for those you can model yourself after, because what you see has a dramatic effect on the life you live.

**Allegiance**

A protégé should have an allegiance to their mentors. Most people have difficulty staying committed for the long haul. Most people get a little color on their paintbrush, make a few strokes and then put the brush down. We are so quick to think we have arrived. Yet a good mentor is worth your total dedication. A mentor provides the insight and hands on experience that you need to succeed. While you are in your time of preparation, learn all that you can. Stay committed to the tutors and coaches in your life until you have the experience, knowledge, wisdom, and maturity it takes to carry out your life's purpose.

## 3. Be Courageous

Determine that you are going to stick to a purposeful way of living no matter what. Don't allow critics to shake your beliefs concerning what you are called to do. Trust in a bright future for you despite any circumstances that arise. You are well able to come out on top! Planning and taking purposeful action daily is the best thing you can do to live a meaningful life that you enjoy. You'll be more confident and less afraid of the paths you must take to success. Be excited about your future. Applaud yourself for being courageous and sticking to a life of purpose and dream achievement. *That's certainly worth celebrating.*

# CREATE A COLLAGE

**Designing My Life to Enjoy:**

## Planning a Purposeful Life

Use the layout on the following page to design your vision in this area. Get glue sticks, magazines and cut out words and pictures to create an Enjoy Life Collage.

What can you do to ensure that you stay focused on your dreams? According to your purpose, decide what type of mentors you need. Make a collage that illustrates the steps you will take to plan purposefully.

Designing a Life to Enjoy
# CREATE A COLLAGE
LifeCoach2Women.com

# CHAPTER 3

# Enjoy

## Goal Setting

*"The world stands aside to let anyone pass who knows where they're going."*
*– David Starr Jordan*

The quest for a life full of meaning and happiness transcends all boundaries of race, denomination, culture, class, or creed. Every person wants to be happy. However they personally define success, everyone wants a taste of it. Those who are courageous dare to dream of being extraordinary; they want to become high achievers. Still the daunting questions seem to be "how do I make it happen? How do I make my life a success?"

The answer to this age-old question is unbelievably simple: set goals.

Regardless of the type, quantity, or magnitude of your dreams, you will have to set goals to realize them. Goals are essential to living a purpose-filled, successful life. A life void of a master plan leaves no room for hope, happiness, or achievement. Goal-less living is one of the greatest acts of self-limitation. It is important that we fill our purpose to be good examples to our families, friends and in your community. Setting goals makes this possible. When we decide not to set or pursue goals, we waste the abilities given to us and the opportunities orchestrated for us.

**How do we find goals?**

You can define your goals by listing human attributes that you admire and working toward incorporating those attributes into your character. Or, you could make a list of challenges in your life and set goals to solve them. However, the main source of your goals comes from your life's mission. A goal is simply a portion of your mission put on a time line.

**Write your goals down**

Things that are written become accessible. My goals are

listed in my *Success Journal and Millionaire's Dream Book* and I review them often. Each year I am amazed at how much I have achieved. Begin by writing down your dreams and desires. Itemize them. Then ask yourself questions, so that you can break your goals down into manageable tidbits. Next, add a deadline. For example, if one of my desires is to lose weight, I must next ask, "how much?" I want to lose thirty pounds. Now my question is, "what does it take to lose thirty pounds?" Answer: Healthy eating and proper exercise. Now I can set a few goals. For example:

Goal: Lose 30 lbs

Goal: Exercise more

Goal: Eat healthier meals

**Stop and write down 5 goals that are important to you right now.**

1. _____
2. _____
3. _____
4. _____
5. _____

The journey to enjoy successful living doesn't end there. You must make a written plan to achieve your goals. For a moment let's return to the simple illustration of my goal to lose 30lbs. Yet again I must ask myself questions. If I found that my goal to lose weight requires proper eating and exercise, I must carefully map out my plan to follow through.

**Take a look:**
Goal: Exercise
Plan: Read exercise magazines. Make a workout schedule. Hire a personal trainer. Purchase workout equipment for home, etc.

Goal: Eat Healthy
Plan: Read about healthy meal plans and edit grocery shopping lists for more healthful purchases. Find healthy ways to cook your favorite dishes.

Follow through is where many people drop out. They begin their quest on hype. But on this journey, hype alone is unfruitful. You need directions and a plan to reach the goal. Look at the list of goals you have written, start now to find out what it takes to achieve them, and begin to develop your plan. The remainder of this chapter will serve as a Motivation Map that will guide you in your crusade to meet your goals. Follow the directions carefully, and you will be sure to reach success. The following is a list of directions to help you turn towards achievement.

### 1. Become Fascinated with the Project

Become fascinated with your projects. When you do, you make a personal investment in the task and feel charged and exuberant. I've heard great leaders say, "You are able to summon up as much energy as it takes to complete the job. Because the energy you invest is repaid by results and positive feedback." The more you love something, the more energy you create to dedicate to it. Consequently, you will be more creative. It takes determination and commitment to accomplish anything. Be prepared to stick to your guns.

When I'm working on a project, I am determined to see it through to completion. I stick to it until I get into a flow. I have to reach my flow, because this is when my thinking is clear, ideas are popping, my energy level is higher, and I have a consistent surge of concentration. Within the "project zone," I am very productive, I make few mistakes and my creativity level is at an all time high. Do you know your flow? Hang in there until you reach it.

### 2. Locate your Personal Prime Time

Discover the time frame of your productive hours. Mine are early in the morning. Every person has an inner clock by which they operate. There are certain times of the day that you work best. Are you an early bird or a midnight owl? Being a morning person, I journalize before my family awakes, so that I am alone with my thoughts. Making the most of the morning, unless I have no choice, I schedule all of my appointments before noon.

**I've provided a little quiz to help you identify your best and worst times throughout the day. Answer the following questions and locate your**

## *Personal* PRIME TIME.

---

1. Which word best describes your AM attitude?
   a.   Alert and ready to go
   b    Passive
   c.   Bitter

2. What type of event would be more enjoyable for you to host?
   a.   A Brunch
   b.   Luncheon
   c.   A Dinner Party

3. What time would you be more likely to take a short nap?
   a.   7pm
   b.   1pm
   c.   8am

4. Your morning shower is a chance for you to:
   a.   Review your to-do list and problem solve
   b.   Listen to music
   c.   Try to wake up

5. At what time would you schedule yourself to sit through a 2-hour workshop?
   a.   Morning
   b.   Afternoon
   c.   Evening

**RESULTS:**

YOU ARE A MORNING GLORY IF YOU ANSWERED "A" TO 3 OR MORE QUESTIONS. YOUR EFFECTIVE TIME IS IN THE AM

.

IF YOU ANSWERED "B" TO THREE OR MORE, YOUR PERSONAL BEST IS SEEN IN THE AFTERNOON.

FOR THOSE OF YOU WHO CHOSE "C" FOR 3 OR MORE, YOU HAVE A NOCTURNAL FLAIR AND YOUR MOST PRODUCTIVE TIME IS AT NIGHT.

NOW THAT YOU KNOW YOUR PRIME TIME, TRY TO PLAN YOUR MEETINGS, PRESENTATIONS, AND SOCIAL EVENTS ACCORDINGLY.

## 3. Brainstorm

This is the act of putting two or more people together to generate ideas or solve a problem simultaneously. Brainstorming takes advantage of collective minds. One person's idea triggers another and so on. A single mind can only do so much!

Create a list of people who you could collaborate ideas with. I often gather my staff for brainstorming meetings. We review new products, plan events, and discover work solutions for the office. As a team they have become inter-dependent on one another's creativity; so a brainstorming meeting always provides a surge of energy for our office.

## 4. Get A Hold of your Time

The person who controls their time, controls their life. Always begin your day with a to-do list. You must prioritize your activities and stay focused. Schedule your phone calls and avoid idle conversations. Evaluate the demands of others, (except your boss during work hours) and steer clear of impromptu meetings with colleagues (or neighbors). I don't allow door-to-door salesman or interest groups to occupy my Saturday afternoons. If I'm entertaining in my home, eating dinner, or spending time with my family, I don't take phone calls. I fiercely guard every minute of every day. To accomplish anything in life you must become extremely protective of your time. Don't waste portions of your life on unhealthy relationships and unproductive pursuits. Locate your true friends, discover your purpose-driven passions, and then begin to edit your life. Don't spend precious time on people or pastimes that are unfruitful and drain your energy. It is more valuable than money, don't let it slip away unused.

## 5. Rescue Yourself from a Rut

To enjoy goal setting and great achievement you cannot remain stagnant. I always evaluate myself to see how I can improve. If you find yourself losing momentum, don't let a lack of progress turn into a state of emergency. However, should you ever become stuck, apply these "self-rescue tactics" immediately, and start your life afresh in the morning.

- **Rescue Tactic 1: Take the Leading Role and Behave Like the Star You Are**
  Though you may not be comfortable focusing totally on your needs, zooming in on you will help you get your bearings. Don't worry about the behavior of others. I've learned that you

can't control anyone but yourself and that's the best place to begin.

- **Rescue Tactic 2: To Thine Own Self be True**
Everything you do is subject to opinions, but don't let that be to your ruin. 'Tis true that there is safety in the multitude of counsel, but don't get your counsel from critics. I don't listen to critics; they always sit on the bench and tell everyone else how to play the game of life. No matter what, just play hard, stay committed to what's right, and don't allow others to define you. Don't be so concerned with competition that you constantly look over your shoulder. That will only slow you down. You'll begin to rise and win as you look straight ahead and press toward the mark.

- **Rescue Tactic 3: Don't Waste Your Evenings**
Make good use of your evenings. When you are in the proverbial "rut" you are more prone to engage in tension relieving activities like television watching and eating. Yet what you do in your free time may mean the difference between the good life and a pathetic

existence. Pull yourself up by closing the fridge, turning off the TV, and investing your free time in learning activities, personal development, and goal achievement. I try to do some kind of industrious activity each night and I always read in the bed before I fall asleep. Don't waste your prime time watching others fulfill their dreams while yours slowly fades away. Now that you know how to get out of a rut, don't ever allow your life to stay stuck.

## 6. Keep Your Confidence

We're coming 'round the mountain with our goals in tow, but you cannot allow the bandits of low-self esteem and a lack of confidence to steal everything you've been working toward. My confidence in my abilities helps me maintain my motivation to succeed. You too must be confident in your ingenuity to accomplish your goals. The following are a few points to help you keep your confidence.

### Confidence Keeper: Consider your progress

You must believe in yourself and showcase your positive traits while building up your weaker ones. Goals are wonderful because they help you to reasonably measure your progress. Stop and recognize the progress you have made and don't give up. You will continue to feel good about yourself as you work on your goals bit by bit.

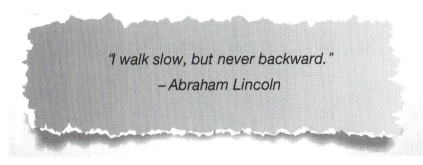

*"I walk slow, but never backward."*
*– Abraham Lincoln*

**Confidence Keeper: Tolerate the mistakes that lead to success**

Colonel Sanders received 1,000 rejections before someone acknowledged his great chicken recipe for the now legendary KFC.

Thomas Edison made 2,000 attempts before the light bulb was actually created.

Abraham Lincoln lost eight elections before he made history with the presidential term he did serve.

Phenomenal success is usually preceded by numerous "failures." Cut yourself some slack if you've made a few mistakes.

**Confidence Keeper: Be grateful**

Count your blessings and be thankful for the sum total. Appreciate the abilities you do have and each day you are given to use them. Each day I am thankful for everything I have. Being ungrateful weakens your ability to value your life and yourself. You will increase your confidence as you refuse to focus on what you don't have, and commit to an attitude of gratitude.

**Confidence Keeper: Redo your body lingo**

Did you know that poor posture is a sign of low self-esteem? Studies show that slumped shoulders and hanging your head demonstrates a lack of confidence. So, straighten up and put your shoulders back. Hold your head up high. Walk like royalty with a confident stride and a faster pace. Higher self-esteem is sure to follow.

**Confidence Keeper: Have the resolve to solve**

Never look at your situation as hopeless. Do your best to solve the problem. Instead of replaying past mistakes like a broken record, ask yourself, "What can I do to make it right?" Imagine what the people you look up to would do if they were in your shoes. There is a solution out there. It's always too soon to quit.

## 7. Reward Yourself: The Final Frontier

Finally, you have written your goals, created a plan, been rescued from a rut, and increased your confidence. You realize success is a journey but you've decided to enjoy it. Now what? REWARD YOURSELF! My husband taught me that whenever I reach a goal to use a portion of my earnings to reward myself. "That will help you avoid burnout;" he says. It's true!

Research at the University of South Carolina at Columbia found that people who reward themselves for even the small steps find it easier to change and improve their life-style. Pat yourself on the back every once and awhile and you'll be motivated to go a little further.

Make a list of things that you want (the items should vary from great to small). Each time you accomplish a goal, choose from the list and treat yourself. Be reasonable though. If one of your goals is to get out of debt, after paying off one bill, it is probably unwise to treat yourself to a 7-day getaway to Tahiti. Begin an "I did it" savings account to provide yourself with life's little treasures as you strive toward your goals.

Rewarding yourself shows that you take yourself seriously even when others do not.

*"I feel that the greatest reward for doing is the opportunity to do more."*
*– Jonas Stalk*

Goal setting will cause you to enjoy the life you were meant to lead. It will help you celebrate who you are and what you are called to do as you strive toward purposeful living. My goals are like magnets. They pull me in the direction of my desired results. Try it. Get out and do more. New experiences lead to new inspiration and new opportunities. The world is at your fingertips. Set your goals and enjoy!

# CREATE a COLLAGE

Designing My Life to Enjoy:

## Goal Setting

**Use the layout on the following page to design your vision in this area. Get glue sticks, magazines and cut out words and pictures to create an Enjoy Life Collage.**

What would your written goals look like in picture form? Do you see the end results in your head, but need a tangible illustration to stimulate you? Create a goal-setting page that brings your goals to life. Then, choose 50 goals from your 101 Goals List in your *Success Journal*. The more you have written down, the more you will achieve.

Designing a Life to Enjoy
# CREATE A COLLAGE
LifeCoach2Women.com

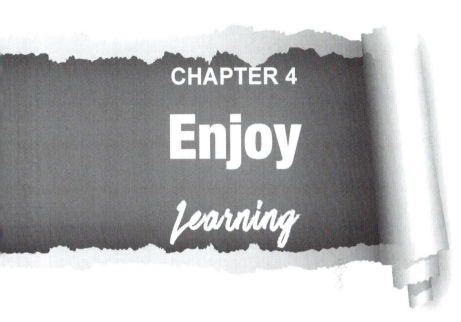

# CHAPTER 4

# Enjoy

## *Learning*

*"Nothing in life is to be feared. It is only to be understood."*
*– Marie Curie, Scientist*

If I told you that I knew a secret process that I guaranteed would help you make more money, look great, get promoted, change careers, upgrade your social status, and be personally fulfilled, would you try it? Would you enjoy your life after making all of those improvements? Though this miracle process is not actually a secret, it is not as widely used, as it should be. The process is called learning, and it can improve your life immensely. Life becomes so much more satisfying when there is a constant flow of learning. Learning is about making the most of the opportunities made available to you, which empowers you to live a life that is more exciting and wonderful than you ever imagined. Developing, enriching, and reinventing one's life has become the mantra of our society today. What you don't know can greatly hinder your success in life. You must get informed. People experience lack, miss opportunities, and even lose their lives, just because they don't have the proper information. Anyone who expects to keep up with the pace of a technologically advanced, well traveled, highly connected, excessively informed world, must expose themselves to lifelong learning. With the rate of technology changing so rapidly, we need to learn new things on a regular basis.

The right information is necessary for financial increase, job advancement, business and even relating to our children (they learn so fast these days). This does not mean that you must go to the closest university and sign over your life for enrollment. What it does mean is that you should always be a student in life. Learning must be weaved into your daily practice.

*I will help you master the process of learning by sharing my tricks of the trade and the principles of learning that all successful people practice.*

# Why Learn?

## 1. To upgrade your standard of living

I hate mediocrity; it's a second-class existence. You were not created to live that way. You do not have to settle for average living. You can makeover your entire life with learning. All you have to do is gain the missing information you need to move forward.

## 2. To expand your mind

The more you learn, the more your view of life expands. As your mentality broadens, you will see more opportunities and have the confidence to set bigger goals. As I grow, my confidence level grows. It becomes easier for me to attempt a new task or take on new ventures. I've found the more that I learn, the more stimulating my conversations become. No longer do I fear carrying on a conversation with intellectual people whom I admire. Do you want to see the same transformation take place in you? Then go on a life-long learning plan. You don't have to tolerate your shortcomings. Join the learning revolution and reinvent yourself.

Oliver Wendell Holmes, a famous writer, once said: "Man's mind, once stretched by a new concept, never regains its original dimension." That's an awesome thought; the minute you add something to your knowledge bank your mind is forever expanded.

### How Can I Learn More?

**Constantly Expand Your Mind with Reading.** The habit of reading is absolutely life changing. You can find the answer to difficult issues and information to help you through tough times in books, magazines, and other great materials. Take inventory of your life and pinpoint what you need to know to get where you want to go. When I tell others about learning, it's natural to talk about reading since it's one of our main resources for personal growth.

Mark Twain said it well, "The man who does not read good books, has no advantage over the man who can't read them."

Reading is so exciting because, not only does it expand our knowledge base, but also it fuels our own ideas and creative work. To make your reading experience more enjoyable, begin reading with curiosity, looking for new ideas. Find strategies you can instantly implement into your life. Write down action steps you can take from what you've learned. If you will begin to read with this kind of enthusiasm and energy, the task of reading will begin to be profoundly meaningful.

Begin the new discipline of reading. You will miss outstanding opportunities because of a lack of knowledge if reading is not a part of your daily life. Make an investment in yourself and your future. Purchase learning materials, CDs, mp3s and especially books, even audio books. Be aware of what they are worth to your lifestyle.

Reading has extensive benefits and a positive impact on the quality of your life. It is a grave mistake to base such investment decisions solely on price. You get what you pay for. The next time you must make a purchasing decision, ask yourself: "Will this information help me to improve or turn my life around?" If the answer is yes, note the value and go for it. The materials are worth every penny.

**The Practice of Reading:**
-Enhances your creativity
-Boosts your vocabulary and knowledge of grammar
-Causes you to be a better thinker
-Makes you evaluate yourself
-Challenges you to make positive changes
-Expands your goals
-Increases your knowledge and awareness of the world
-Broadens your interests and satisfies your curiosity
-Ignites you to generate new ideas

**How to annotate & highlight when you read:**
-Highlight new words and major points
-Bracket key passages
-Write new words to add to your vocabulary. Put them at the top of the page
-Star important facts
-Write numbers to order things you read about in sequence
-Put a question mark by the things you don't understand or disagree with.
-Summarize key paragraphs in the margins
-Use your *Success Journal* to write down your action steps.

-List the things you want to apply to your life from your readings.

**10 Great Points to Sharpen Your Reading Skills:**

1. Set aside time each day for silent reading of things that you are interested in.

2. If you have trouble reading, get help! Take some reading comprehension courses. Take an English class. Don't be afraid to go back to school or take a course! Hire yourself a tutor if necessary.

3. Be curious about new words. Get a dictionary and try to learn a word a month. The more you learn the better reader you will be.

4. Watch educational TV shows or videos.

5. Be a take-charge reader. Conquer reading a book that is a little difficult for you.

6. Be aware of your level of understanding. Wise people can identify where they really are, and do something about it.

7. Visit the library. Get yourself a library card if you don't already have one. Spend a day researching a topic of interest.

8. Keep track of the books you read in a reading log, a book report form, or in a journal. I use the Book Notes section in my *Success Journal* so I have the information at my fingertips.

9. Vary your reading. Try magazines, biographies, poetry, dictionaries, or possibly a novel.

10. Read aloud to a younger child.

## Hunting & Gathering

Enjoyment is found in discovery. There is bliss in hunting and gathering. Everyday you can collect bits of information by always carrying something to read with you. I keep a book or magazine in my purse, so I can take advantage of waiting time. While at the airport, the dentist office, before a meeting, in the car etc., all of those little glimpses of time add up. To collect information, begin by making a list of topics that interest you. Buy some file folders and label them with your topics of interest. Next time you are reading, begin collecting articles, statistics, and quotes and make notes on your subjects of interest.

## What To Do With Your Findings

With new information you expand your possibilities. You can start a business, discover your purpose, become a better parent, enhance your work skills, discover a new invention, or even write a book. Look closely, you'll find it. At one of my live events a lady shared how she applied this principle and started a home organization business. I was told that this wonderful lady heard me speak about collecting information on your topic of interest. This fountain of information led to the idea of opening a home organization business. Her hunting and gathering not only led to fulfilling life work, but great financial increase.

# Make Use of Learning Locations

### Learn from Travel

When you travel, you leave your comfort zone, which ignites your curiosity to explore new things. Keep a travel journal to record all that you learn. Better yet, check out *Around the World in Style: Travel Journal* by Ariana Pierce. While looking through my travel journal, I've learned about different cultures and foods noticing that I have had a vast amount of dining experiences. My journal is filled with outstanding specialty stores, tips on decorating gathered from hotels, and customer service do's and don'ts from many outings. I also cut out pictures of places that I desire to travel to.

### Learn While in Commute

Audio books and audio learning lessons from seminars or conferences are an easy way to get new information.

### Learn from Other People

Without sounding like an investigative reporter, ask a few questions of someone more knowledgeable than you, in your field of interest. When you're in the presence of someone with advanced knowledge, asking questions will increase your awareness about a particular subject. Here are a few pointers to help you learn from those you converse with.

- *Ask the question; then allow the person to respond.*
- *Have a notebook handy; write down what's being said.*
- *If you didn't get a complete understanding from their response, ask them to elaborate and explain a little further.*
- *After all of your questions have been answered, summarize what you've heard.*

## Learn During Leisure-Time

Learning is continual, so don't try to wait until you've "learned enough" to finally have some fun. Enjoy life now. Even while you are in pursuit of a better life, learning can be a blast!

### Fun ways to learn:

- *Play games with your kids*
- *Play scrabble or other word games*
- *Play Monopoly or Hot Company (learn business)*
- *Work on crossword puzzles*
- *Play travel games in the car i.e. name all the states and their capital cities.*

# *Start Your Own* Kiddie College

Researchers say that despite studies at school, the most vital learning takes place at home. Start your own "Kiddie College" with these star techniques to help your children become A+ learners.

**1**. Encourage your kids to love learning. Do fun learning activities and make learning commonplace in your home. Then, children will associate learning with positive experiences and be less likely to fear what it takes to discover new information.

**2**. Have just reading time. Turn off all the electronics and phones.

**3**. Purchase books on every topic that they enjoy.

**4**. Challenge them periodically for expanding their knowledge.

**5**. Reward them periodically for expanding their knowledge.
**6**. Be an example. When they see that you love to learn, they will most likely follow your lead.

# *Easy Ways to Stay* 'On the Grow'

**1. Learn From the Best Not Just the Accessible**
Seek out people who know what they are doing, and who have performed at high standards on a consistent basis for a period of time. Invest in books and information by people you want to learn from. Never leave the presence of a well-educated person without trying to increase your knowledge.

**2. Consistently Improve**
Keep improving yourself by applying what you have learned. Take some kind of action within 24 hours after you learn something new.

**3.  Face the Facts**
Be real with yourself about what areas you need to become educated in. You cannot correct what you are unwilling to confront. There is no shame in having to learn something. Refusing to learn new things is what is shameful.

**4. Adjust your Daily Routine**
The secret of your future is hidden in your daily routine. Is learning a part of your daily routine?

**5. Learn Like You're Preparing for Something**

The quality of your preparation determines the quality of your performance. Do research before you make a major move.

**6. Turn your Learning into Dreams and Goals**

As you gather and receive new information, write down ways you will activate what you have heard into your life through written dreams and goals.

**7. Learn How to be Promoted**

You will never be promoted until you have become overqualified for your present position. That means spending time "overlearning," studying, practicing, and gathering.

**8. Store up Knowledge**

Prepare for an opportunity that doesn't exist yet. Keep learning because eventually a door will open to use what you have been gathering.

**9. Become a "Techie"**

Learn about all of the new and exciting things that today's technology has to offer. Learn to use the Internet and social media, and you'll wonder how you ever knew anything without it. Get educated about all of the new lifestyle management gadgets. For instance, I have an iPad, which is great for a multitude of daily tasks. I tell my clients to invest in the latest tech toys so that they can be just as productive. Tablets, smart phones, etc. are great substitutes when you don't want to lug around your laptop. Plus they're light and easier to travel with when you're on the road.

**10. Learn to Take Good Notes**
Your mind only remembers 6% of what it hears even after hearing the same information multiple times. Therefore, it is imperative that you equip yourself for improvement by taking good notes.

*Why Take Notes?*

1. Writing things down reinforces what you hear and helps you remember.

2. Taking notes makes you a more active listener.

3. Note taking skills are critical for getting information to succeed in life.

4. Taking notes helps you to communicate clearly and give top-notch performance.

All of our staff members are required to take notes when they talk to my husband and I. What we say to them is very important. Note taking insures that they have clear instructions. Then, we usually ask them to repeat back to us what we assigned them to do. Likewise, if you receive instruction on a daily basis, you should have a planner for note taking.

## How to Take Good Notes:

o Date your notes.
o Give your notes a title.
o Use a notebook worth keeping. Invest in quality products.
o Number or letter your points.
o Leave some blank space to fill in other ideas.
o Make note of the main ideas that come to you and make them stand out from the other text or notes.
o List all important details.
o Follow up on your notes in the next few days. Review and revise them, transfer information to journals, *Success Journal*, etc.
o Tell someone what you learned. Sharing helps you remember.
o Take action and apply what you have learned.

# How to Maximize Your Ability to Learn

1. **Invest Time.** Sometimes you may have to get up earlier or stay up later to learn something new.

2. **Get Learning Music.** You'll be surprised at how many ideas come to you while listening to the music of Mozart or other classical composers. Listen to music while you are commuting.

3. **Create an Environment Conducive for Learning.** Surround yourself with good books, play stimulating music, keep your desk supplied with study materials e.g. highlighters, pens, paper, a dictionary, a journal, and file folders. Turn off the TV.

4. **List the Topics That Interest You.** What do you want to learn about the topic? How much time are you currently spending increasing your knowledge of this subject? Write down what you are currently learning that's new and refreshing.

5. **Find Friends That Help You Grow.** Be accountable to a motivational friend who is always learning something new themselves. Brainstorm with other creative minds for ideas.

**6. Be Optimistic.** You can do it! It's time to makeover your life with learning. Read, Absorb, and Apply. You're headed toward the best days of your life.

> *"Learning is exciting! It's like being on the edge of something that is being reinvented."*
> *– Dr. Stacia Pierce*

**7. Learn to Love it.** As you plunge yourself into your self-improvement efforts, you will develop a love for learning. You'll cherish how you feel when you're "in the know." It is a privilege to be able to learn, so enjoy it.

**8. Join the Learning Revolution.** You don't have to stay average. Now, go on a learning spree! Buy audios, books, and journals to record your notes. Get highlighters and pens that you really like. Gather your educational treats and prepare to excel.

**9. Face the Challenge of Promotion.** Take calculated risks based on your "inner cues" and the information that you have gathered. If you have set your sights on a new position or career, make a plan and go for it.

*"Always Stay on the Grow!"*
*– Dr. Stacia Pierce*

### Road Rules for Career Changing:

1. Save money and research while you are still employed. Put "rainy day" money on reserve while you find out what experience you need for your new job.

2. Work Quickly to Build a Network. I'll preface this by saying DO NOT steal your present employer's contacts. Just be mindful of the type of people you need to know for your next career. Who you have access to is important to your success. Investigate how you can locate and meet people in the field that you want to go into.

3. Give Yourself a Deadline. Write your goals; then face the reality of your situation. How long can you afford to be "in transition"? Sometimes it may be

necessary to get a "filler job" until you are able to get into the field you want.

4. Attack! Don't be passive about your dreams. Work hard. Give it all you got and look forward to awesome results.

# CREATE A COLLAGE

Designing My Life to Enjoy

## Learning

**Use the layout on the following page to design your vision in this area. Get glue sticks, magazines and cut out words and pictures to create an Enjoy Life Collage.**

Is there a subject that peaks your curiosity? Is there a business that you want to start and need to learn more about? Are you in need of more information to solve a problem? You can do it! Create a collage page that sparks your "how to" ideas.

Designing a Life to Enjoy
# CREATE A COLLAGE
LifeCoach2Women.com

# CHAPTER 5

# Enjoy

*Keeping an Enjoy Life Journal*

> *"Even human life has the potentiality of becoming an art work."*
> *– Ira Progoff*

Creators of sculptures, paintings, clothing, films, jewelry or any other work that increases in value, all have a place to preserve their thoughts, ideas, philosophies, and plans. Whether it's a drafting table, a story board, a sketch book, or a blank canvas, every extraordinary work has its beginning on paper. Keeping an "Enjoy Life Journal," provides you with a place to begin your design for exceptional living. Picture this journal as your creativity canvas. Your ingenious ideas, jolts of information, crafty finds, and inspiring moments can all be captured on the precious pages of your journal. A good life is planned. We have to tend to the details if we want to live a joyful life. Your journal is your life-planning book. Using a journal is one of the most effective ways to ensure a meaningful and enjoyable life. Journalizing has been an essential part of my daily routine for years. Written here is the journalizing insight that has helped me to strategize my life's plans. I'm sure that as you apply these practices, your life will become more peaceful, productive, and purposeful!

## How to Make the Most of Your Journal

### Be Prepared

Carry a pen and paper with you at all times. Jot down anything that positively affects you. Recount a story you heard, a good book you've read, or a significant conversation with a friend. Look out your window and really enjoy your flower garden. Then sit down once or twice a week to compose these thoughts into journal entries. If you don't happen to have a pen and note jotter, then your smart phone may work just as well. Install a good notes app on your phone, and write out your thoughts there.

**Have Great Expectations**

I've found that wisdom speaks more when you are looking for it and are prepared for answers to come. Journalizing is really double sided; it is writing as well as listening. When you take out your pen and paper to journalize, anticipate hearing the voice of wisdom and open your heart to listen.

**Capture Your Thoughts in Action**

Record answers to your questions or witty ideas and inventions that come to you. Whether it's in the middle of the night or early in the morning capture your inspired thoughts in action. I can look back through my journals and realize that what I've written was more than just my thoughts. They were words and phrases that related to my core purpose. My writings are at times revelatory, and I am thankful that they are captured in my journal.

**Know your Journal Preferences**

Use what appeals to you. A special journal with nice paper, along with a unique and comfortable pen, will set the tone for your writing. Find a journal that fits your personality and your situation. Choose a design that is inspiring and pleasing to the eye. Simply picking up your journal should encourage you to write. When I am writing my most private thoughts at home, I use a rather expensive journal. I love the luxury of holding the soft colorful suede cover as I record the sweetest moments of my life.

## Become a Buyer of Empty Books

Invest in journals that you will enjoy writing in. When making your entries, use beautiful pens, markers, crayons, or colored pencils. Gel pens are my favorites. I'm sure I own one in every color they make. Feel free to use the kind of writing instruments that you love. You are the artist and your journal is the canvas.

## Absorb and Observe Life

Document your enlightenment in your journal. You will find that one discovery will lead to another. Don't let your memories slip away. If need be, turn your journal into somewhat of a scrapbook. When I want to make note of an important event, I try to have some memorabilia. I keep the ticket stubs and program cover to insert on my journal pages.

## Go to the Writing Room

Find a place that you call your writing room. It can be your bedroom, living room, sunroom, or even a spot in your garden. Walk through your home and locate your favorite spot to write. Store your favorite writing instruments there. Each time you journalize, go to that spot and select a pen that suits your mood. By making this a habit, you will find you are calmer and more prepared to record your thoughts.

### Be Honest

Effective journalizing requires you to be honest and truthful. Your journal is your personal outlet. Don't hold back when writing your thoughts, activities, or insights. Nothing is too silly or unimportant to write down. Your wit and wisdom is worth recording. Keep in mind that your journal is not a diary. Don't use it to vent and share your ill feelings. Write what you desire and look forward to, your inner most thoughts. Later, when you read through your journal, you will discover that your words were more meaningful than you imagined. By using this process, you will be able to review your life and discover where you need to add splashes of joy.

### Give Your Journal Positive Headings

Sharing even the most dreadful news can be done from a positive angle. Motivate yourself by writing a positive heading at the top of each journal page. This way you will be more likely to extract and record the happy moments of your day.

### The Compliment List

Use your journal to remind yourself of the kind things that others say about you. Designate a place within your

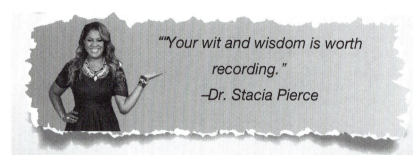

journal to document all of the compliments people give you. It's an easy pick-me-up when you're feeling a bit blue or under the weather.

### Write your Way to a Brighter Day

Every night, write in your journal what you want the next day to be like. Write specific things you want to happen for you. We have not because we ask not. Often I write questions in my journal at night and by the morning, I have the answer (either by way of a dream or a still small voice upon my wakening). Even if your answer doesn't sound with the alarm clock, be patient a solution is on the way.

Writing in a journal helps you to preserve good memories and keeps you in touch with your inner most feelings. I am grateful for all of the things in my life. When I have had a truly eventful week, weekend, or day, I record what made the time so special. Developing the discipline of journalizing helps you gain more understanding and opens your life up to possibilities. As you enjoy your life be sure to journalize. Remember, your wit and wisdom is worth recording.

# Journalizing Resources

Keep a Success Journal. Try it for the next 30 days, and I promise you will be amazed at the results.

Here are a few suggestions to get you started.

1. Describe a wonderful place you've traveled to and the way it made you feel.
2. What are your favorite things to do? How does it make you feel?
3. Write down at least five things you love about yourself.
4. As fast as you can, write a list of the things you are thankful for.
5. Think of a person who has made a positive difference in your life. How and why did they impact your life? Have you ever told them what they have done for you?
6. What is your favorite restaurant? What do you enjoy about dining there?
7. What songs motivate you? Write them down. Make sure you have them available in your home and car.
8. Think of two authors who have inspired you in some way. Write down how they inspired you.

9. If there were no money or time constraints, what would you do with your life right now? Record it.
10. Make a list of what you're just putting up with in life. Include everything big or small. Now vow to remove each thing you merely tolerate as soon as possible.
11. Record all your achievements. i.e. like a well-done project, a class you completed, a new dish you cooked well, or a problem you solved. Whatever has given you a feeling of accomplishment, write it down.
12. Create a list of all the places you would like to travel to in the next five years.
13. What physical activities would you like to try? (i.e. biking, running, swimming, tennis). List them all, ignore your inhibitions, and make plans to do them soon.
14. Who is your favorite person to be around? Why are they special, and what do you do together?
15. If you could remodel your house and spare no expense, what changes would you make? Describe in detail. You never know what ideas will emerge.
16. Pretend you were starting a business. What would it be called? What service would you provide? Design your business card.
17. If you are married, when was the last time you wrote your husband a love letter? Write one in your journal first. Then, find a creative card or pullout your best stationery. Rewrite the letter and send it to him.
18. Write your children a motivational letter of love and encouragement. Do this in your journal first, for safekeeping. Then, compose it again and mail it to them.

19. With whom do you laugh at the most? Write about a time you laughed so hard, that you couldn't stop. Spend more time with the person who makes you laugh.
20. Write down one thing you've been meaning to do when you had time. Start right now.
21. What are your favorite colors? How often do you use them? How could you incorporate more of them into your life?
22. List the activities you've done in the last year you enjoyed most. Why not add more of them to your schedule?
23. Think of a way you could surprise and delight someone you love tomorrow. Make plans to do so.
24. If you're married, think of five qualities you adore in your mate. If you're single, write a list about a friend. Whoever you wrote about, read them your list tomorrow.
25. Write down three books that have impacted your life and three people you know who would be changed and motivated by them. Now, either purchase the books for them as gifts, or suggest that they buy them.
26.-30. Label the top of five pages with a heading that says "I'm passionate about _____."
Fill in the blanks on each sheet then elaborate on what those titles mean to you.

# CREATE a COLLAGE

**Designing My Life to Enjoy**

## Keeping my Enjoy Life Journal

Use the layout on the following page to design your vision in this area. Get glue sticks, magazines and cut out words and pictures to create an Enjoy Life Collage.

What kind of journals fit your fancy? Where do you like to write? Would you prefer an entire room or a desk on which to journalize? Imagine your ideal setting and create your collage page for journalizing.

*Designing a Life to Enjoy*

# CREATE A COLLAGE
LifeCoach2Women.com

# External

*Clues*

# CHAPTER 6

# Enjoy

## Shopping

*"Outfitting yourself is a true expression of individual style. Shopping, is the means by which that expression is made."*
**– Dr. Stacia Pierce**

Shopping holds many meanings for different people. Some view it as a fashionable odyssey of sensations, colors, sights, sounds, and smells. Some view it as a great hunt; to track down, purchase, and bring home items, which you will showcase as trophies. Others only see it as a means to an end. However you define shopping, it is my desire to stimulate you to engage in new shopping experiences, inspire you to explore, investigate, and learn more about yourself and your personal style. As you read along, you will become armed with the knowledge and information necessary to be a confident, savvy shopper. I want you to discover your sources of joy and vision, and to translate those feelings into your purchases. The art of shopping is about using the things you love to buy to express yourself, and fill up on what fuels you. Shopping is a journey, so let the information provided here help you navigate the way!

Today there are a myriad of different shopping venues and each coincides with the personal style of the shopper. There is the field trip shopper, the Internet shopper, and even the personal shopper (who will bring your purchases right to your home or hotel room). I guess I would call myself a field trip shopper. I like to experience the adventure of it all. I love to get out and explore. It's a break for me to get away from all of my daily responsibilities and rejuvenate my mental muscles by shopping. You should let your interest guide what I call your "leave time." What do you enjoy doing most when you can leave everything else behind? Balanced and content people do what they like to do as often as they can.

Of course, your financial state will determine how much and where you shop. Learn to balance these attributes in order to get the most from your experiences. Don't shop excessively if you can't afford it. I grew up shopping with my Dad every Saturday. So as a teen, it was a way of life. When I became an adult, spending my own money, I put shopping into perspective. In the last few years, I've been blessed and able to shop more than ever. Every woman should master the pleasurable art of shopping. No matter what your style, you've got to admit you enjoy a new purchase every now and again.

No matter how much you enjoy your purchases, if you do not make educated choices when shopping, your wardrobe will still lack the punch and polish that helps you look your best.

Building a well-coordinated wardrobe will help you feel good about yourself every time you step outside of your home. Planning your wardrobe needs careful attention and dressing with each day's events in mind will cause you to express yourself with both confidence and pleasure.

## How to be a Better Shopper

### 1. Set a Budget
Before you ever start your shopping excursion, set some limits. Several months before I go to New York for

my annual shopping binge, I begin putting away money into my shopping fund. That way I have a nice size budget and do not interfere with any of my other financial business.

## 2. Take a Closet Inventory

What pieces do you need? What will update your look? What are your favorite colors? What could give you more outfit combinations? Write everything down in your *Journal* and take it with you on each shopping trip. What accessories do you need to pull together your look?

## 3. Get a Vision

Look through fashion magazines for appealing and current styles. I clip and paste what I like, either in my *Millionaire's Dream Book* or *Success Journal.* Sometimes, I take the pictures on my phone along with me to help me stay on track to purchase what I really want.

## 4. Set Your Shopping Goals

What do you want to accomplish on this trip? Write down what items you want to come home with. This will keep you focused. You can use the *Superstar Chic Fashion Journal* by Ariana Pierce.

### 5. Decide on your Shopping Location

What mall or stores do you want to go to? What are the hours of operation? What's the price range? When I'm planning on shopping out of town, for example, in New York, or Los Angeles, I always try to arrive a day early just to regroup and relax. That way, the next day I'm rested and can hit the stores early in the morning.

### 6. Outfit Yourself for Successful Shopping

Wear your makeup and hair in a way that will complement the type of clothes you are shopping for. Also, wear an outfit that is easy to slip on and off (this is a must for serious shopping days). A lightweight, over the shoulder purse with a long strap is convenient, especially if you're carrying shopping bags too. Comfortable shoes are an absolute necessity.

### 7. Wear Very Nice Underwear

Remember what your mother told you. Always wear fresh underwear that is in good condition. It is much more flattering to try on clothes when your undergarments look beautiful and they fit well.

### 8. Shop Unrestrained

When you plan to do some serious shopping, plan your day well in advance. The worst way to shop is by trying to beat the clock. I leave my day open ended so I can take my time. That's what makes it fun.

## 9. Find the Right Shopping Partner

I have some basic rules. I avoid serious shopping with someone who is not shopping at all. Talk about a thorn in the flesh. Don't shop with someone whose budget limit or clothing tastes are so drastically different from yours. They may offer negative opinions about the styles and prices you choose, which can distort your view. Your shopping partner should be able to go at your pace and like the same kind of stores you do.

## 10. Make Sure Your Clothes Fit

Take time to try on an outfit or pair of shoes you are contemplating purchasing. Items always look different on a display than when actually on your body. Look in the mirror from all angles. Do the clothes fall on your body correctly? Do you like the feel? Be satisfied before you buy; returns are generally a hassle.

# How to Shop for Inspiration

I love to shop because I love the stimulation it provides. The sights, sounds, smells, window displays, and the outfits of fellow shoppers are invigorating. I leave with far more than just a purchase; I bring home inspiration!

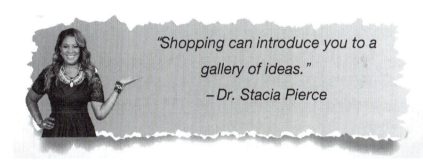

"Shopping can introduce you to a gallery of ideas."
– Dr. Stacia Pierce

### Keep a Shoppers Journal

After an elaborate shopping trip, I like to record everything. Your *Success Journal or Superstar Chic Fashion Journal* is the perfect place to carry around your fabric color swatches, dream looks, shopping lists, and inventory of what you already own. After your trip go home, record the deals that you got, names and numbers of your favorite stores, and anything else that stood out to you. This is good information to record for future shopping trips.

### Keep Your Eyes Open

Always be on the lookout for how other chic shoppers are dressed. Observe what the sales ladies are wearing. You can learn a lot about how to update your image by just strolling through the mall with an absorbing eye.

### Pinpoint Your Personal Pleasure

What little treats from the store fascinate you? Is a fragrance purchase your favorite? If so, spend time at the perfume counter finding out about new perfumes. Whatever you delight in, seek it out. Learn to cultivate what shopping tendencies come naturally to you. When making purchasing choices, go for items that accentuate your unique qualities.

## 10 Practical Reasons Why We *Shop*:

1. Shopping is a pleasurable activity.
2. Shopping satisfies a physical as well as emotional need.
3. Shopping keeps your wardrobe replenished and up to date.
4. Shopping can be a way of bonding with friends.
5. Shopping can introduce you to new ideas and inspiration.
6. Shopping causes you to dream beyond your means and think big.
7. Shopping is a way of pampering yourself and tuning in to your own personal needs.
8. Shopping puts you in a self-discovery mode where you explore your likes, dislikes, colors, and style.
9. Shopping provides visual stimulation and sensory pleasures.
10. Shopping expands your vision and upgrades your personal image.

### Ladies Please Note:

Just because you love shopping doesn't mean you're a compulsive, out of control woman who is trying to escape reality (especially if your reality is that you can afford it). There are those of us who have balanced lives _and_ checkbooks. So be comforted my friends, our love for the mall isn't always a reflection of out of whack priorities.

# My Shopping Stories & Great Ideas

## Friends & Fashion

You can turn your shopping trip into a great adventure when you add a girlfriend or two. Over the past few years, I've changed the way I shop. I've improved my strategy and even started having items shipped home. It saves time when I travel and prevents me from having to carry so much around. Additionally, I have personal shoppers and some of my favorite stores. They set aside things they know I will love and when I can stop in to peek, I look and make selections from what they found for me. Once a good sales person knows your likes, dislikes and size, it is easy for them to hold items according to your taste.

Now that I travel more, I also have my purchases shipped home for me. It makes it like a new surprise when I return from my travels.

## Shopping Mall Slumber Party

Organizing a shopping trip with a lot of ladies can be extremely fun, if done correctly. Years ago I planned a shopping retreat with my team at the fabulous Mall of America in Minnesota. We were chauffeured there by a private chartered bus. While on our way, we all engaged in conversation about fashion and beauty.

The accommodations were lovely and all of the women enjoyed being "roommates for the weekend." The ladies were given an agenda for the week. It was truly a mall party. We snapped pictures, explored all the stores and dined out at upscale restaurants, and all within the confines of the mall.

**Beauty Playgrounds**

I'm fascinated with makeup. It has a powerful ability to make instant improvements. When I'm at the makeup counter, I'm like a child at play. On one outing, I took two of my protégés to the makeup wonderland—the MAC cosmetics store. There they took Beauty Lesson 101. Both of them were very impressed with the array of colors, styles, choices, and makeup tools to choose from. Then we moved to other makeup havens to continue our day of cosmetic play.

The ladies went home with tons of information to fill in their *Success Journals*, such as the importance of skin care, knowing their skin type, etc. They discovered whether they preferred crème lipstick or matte lipstick, they observed how using the proper makeup applicators gives a more defined look. At the conclusion of our day, we all went home with goody bags full of cosmetics. I love visiting makeup stores, I feel like a kid in a candy store, big fun.

## Celebrity Makeover

Very close friends of ours came to spend a weekend with my husband and I. Not long after their anticipated arrival, we quickly paired off to engage in our childhood activities. As the men went off to complete their agenda, I was ready to execute my "girls only plan." Our itinerary included a star-treatment makeover. So off to the mall we went to visit the makeup counter. I told my favorite stylist at the counter, "Give my friend a celebrity makeover, she's a VIP."

After twenty minutes of meticulous application, the stylist had created a masterpiece. My friend and I continued to try several new eye and cheek color options on the back of our hands. I kept stretching her to venture out and wear more color. Craving treats at our next stop, the smoothie shop, I told my stylist, "That's a wrap, I'll take everything she tried on and likes. Package it pretty, it's my gift to her." "Another victory for the girls" I thought, and we continued on our shopping quest.

## Back to School Shopping

Years ago when our kids were in school, our back-to-school shopping ritual was a trip to Chicago. It's not that we couldn't find clothes in our own city, but we wanted to ensure that back-to-school preparations were considered a big deal, so our children would understand that school is ultra important to us, and therefore to them. One year, we decided to upgrade our children's back-to-school shopping trip to the Big Apple. Our entire family headed to Manhattan, New York for a shopping trip extravaganza. Of course, we planned to catch a Broadway show and possibly visit a museum or two. But our main focus was shopping.

In preparation for that trip, my daughter Ariana, pulled out pictures from magazines illustrating the style and look she wanted for school. She had several pages of outfits in her vision book. I outlined our trip in my Journal. During our five-day stay, everyone in my family had different needs to be met. My husband focused on shoes and ties, my daughter looked for comfortable, yet very stylish back-to-school clothes. My son Ryan loved to get dressed up, so he was in search of dress suits so he could look like his Dad. So of course, we shopped for dress clothes for him. As for me, I hunted for an assortment of things—jewelry, shoes, suits, handbags, and of course makeup. In order for everyone to come home happy, I had to design a shopping schedule. When shopping with your whole family, plan wisely to ensure a peaceful, satisfying trip. Now, we head to New York and other destinations several times per year for shopping. We plan our lists every time to ensure full enjoyment and to make sure everyone purchases their desired list.

## Consignment Shopping

If you are still in the beginning stages of discovering your personal style, this method of shopping may not be for you. Women who have mastered their style may find consignment shops a great way to reward themselves with more, while spending less. You should note that vintage shops are not always discounted. Finer vintage clothing may carry a weightier price tag than you think. Bargain or not, if you haphazardly shop for these previously worn or vintage items, you will more than likely emerge looking worn and outdated. Both vintage and consignment shopping is for veteran shoppers with a keen eye.

## Shopping Online

It's a great convenience, but if you're a shopper that lives off the thrill of the hunt, you may not want to count out the mall just yet. I don't deny the ease of online purchasing, but I still need the excitement of uncovering a bargain, trying on the perfect pair of shoes, and getting a perfume sample from the really nice lady at the counter.

On the flip side, online shopping is great for the super efficient shopper (like my mother). She hates shopping with me. Mom claims that I "take too long and am too easily distracted" by ventures other than what we came for in the mall (isn't that what the mall experience is all about?). Consequently, online shopping is a great option for her. She can purchase exactly what she wants, whenever she needs it. With special shopping sites in abundance, you can find almost anything with a keyword search and a few "double clicks."

### Ready, Get Set, Shop!

Now, you are well informed and prepared for shopping and to enjoy the adventure that it is. Enjoy your shopping time and make it an expression of you. Never again purchase something you absolutely don't love. Use each shopping quest as an opportunity to expand your creativity and improve your image. Shopping is about learning, loving yourself, and having "the look." Congratulations, you're on your way to becoming a master shopper. What could be more fun? Happy Hunting!

# CREATE A COLLAGE

Designing My Life to Enjoy:

## Shopping

**Use the layout on the following page to design your vision in this area. Get glue sticks, magazines and cut out words and pictures to create an Enjoy Life Collage.**

Wardrobing dreams can come true. What store would you love to shop in without restraint? Give yourself permission to plan your most exciting shopping trip ever! Create a page that shows your shopping delight.

Designing a Life to Enjoy

# CREATE A COLLAGE
LifeCoach2Women.com

# CHAPTER 7

# Enjoy

## Travel

**"Travel exposes you to new opportunities and opens your imagination to new possibilities."**
**– *Ariana Pierce***

Imagine yourself as an exceptionally posh, globetrotting diva. Your conversation is full of adventure and you exude a well-bred confidence, which intrigues the locals that you chat with. Your dress is very vogue and your beauty is quite cosmopolitan. Who's *that* girl? Is she just a mirage? Not necessarily, it could be you. How you achieve this transformation is by setting your sights on becoming well traveled. Traveling demands that you absorb life in a different way because you are able to break away from your usual routines. Journeys to distant locations (and even those that aren't so distant) enlighten, expand, and challenge our minds; thus building our intelligence and feeding our creativity. The color, sounds, aroma, and tangible surroundings of the places you travel create an imprint on your soul that is unparalleled by any other experience.

I love to travel and have triumphantly turned on my daughter to its joys as well. Throughout the year, Ariana joins me on my traveling excursions. For the first six months we travel the country together while on the Success Tour. As often as possible, I extend our stay a day or two for sightseeing and shopping especially if it's our first time in the city.

This "on the road" experience has been eye opening for both of us. Together, Ariana and I have learned about different cultures, gathered creative decorating ideas, learned about world history, shopped in some of the most outstanding stores, developed new points of view, and absorbed the grandeur of some of the most awesome landscapes ever created. Covering a sizeable piece of the U.S, we've toured the famous homes of literary people, artists, political figures, and successful business leaders.

Enormous amounts of inspiration can be provided by an unexpected chance to observe a street singer, harmonica player, or dancer at work. I've been blessed to watch an artist fill out a blank canvas. Rest from a day of walking by partaking in a five-minute street massage and hear incredibly talented musicians fill the air with delightful melodies on a warm summers night. It's absolute inspiration. No wonder fashion designers, writers, creative directors, CEO's, and many other successful people travel as a means of enjoyment and as a tool to sharpen their creative edge.

Certain cities can spark excitement and provide you with a rush. That's what Manhattan, New York does for me. It's my favorite place. Each time I go, I make a new discovery and leave charged with enthusiasm. A richer more rewarding life can be yours when you enjoy traveling and venturing out into new territory.

*"The glories of traveling abroad can be grasped not just by the hands, but by all senses."*
*– Margaret Russell, Former Editor in Chief, Architectural Digest Magazine*

## Create your Dream Travel List

If you're ready to don your globetrotting gear, the first step you can take is making a dream travel list. Document the places you want to see and then your travel fantasies and turn them into legitimate future plans. *Around the World: The Traveler's Journal* is one of my favorites from Ariana's Style-N-Travel Girl line. It's easy to keep my dream list in my Journal because there is already a page dedicated to it. Pull out your travel journal (or a piece of paper right now) and begin to list all of the places you would like to travel to. If you are using the travel journal, turn next to the Travel To-Do List page, and fill in any specific sights that you dream of seeing.

Your list of sights could include the Eiffel Tower, the Grand Canyon, the Mona Lisa, or the Statue of Liberty. When I created my dream list, it revealed to me what type of traveler I was. Your list will do the same for you.

My top tourist destinations are: Harrod's department store in London, designer houses in Paris, custom suit shops in Japan, and handbag and fashion stores in Italy. When I travel I like to spend time in tea rooms, dine in fine restaurants, see upscale homes, and stay in luxury spas.

After evaluating the places I like to go along with my sightseeing priorities, I came to the conclusion that I am a very sophisticated traveler.

My assistant's list is nothing like mine. She dreams of travel excursions that include all kinds of adventures. So her list reveals that she is a very adventurous person. After you write a dream travel list, study it. The locations you want to see will help reveal your travel personality and what activities will make your life more enjoyable.

Periodically, take out your travel list and review what you have written. As new interests arise, add them to your list. This syllabus of your desired trips marks the beginning of your new life with travel and fun adventures.

### Frame Your Travel Future

It is now time to use your imagination to turn your dream trips into reality. Get out your *Millionaire's Dream Book*, and go to one of the travel pages. On this page create a visual collage with words and images that express your specific dreams. Gather travel brochures, advertisements, and magazines. A few of my favorite magazines for travel photos and information are *National Geographic, Conde Nast Traveler,* and *Gourmet.* You can also call a travel agency and ask for pictorial brochures of your future destinations or go online and print out pictures that you love. After you've collected most of your literature, begin to cut out pictures and words of your desired destinations, paste up your collage, and refer to it again and again.

### Keep Travel Files

At this stage, you are getting pretty serious about enjoying a life full of extraordinary travel experiences, so it's time to do what the pro's do. Purchase colorful loose file folders or an accordion file to keep all of your travel information in. Label each folder with every destination on your list. You are now prepared to collect data on your dream trips. If you read a magazine and come across an informative article about an outstanding restaurant in a city or country you plan to visit; clip it and put it into your files. If a friend travels before you do to one of your dream destinations, have them bring postcards or literature from sights they visited, and put them in your file. Date all your files so you know how current the information is. Get travel books on the destinations you plan to attend. Take notes from the books, and put them away in your files.

I've taught my daughter to keep files of her travel destinations as well. She has created her files from magazines, TV shows, and of movies she's seen. On a trip to New York when my daughter was very young, she had an article about the restaurant Serendipity that she had clipped. Serendipity is an eclectic little restaurant that is famous for its huge desserts and as a hangout for many teen stars. Her dream came true when we ate there our first night in Manhattan. Now, Ariana takes speaking engagements around the world. She sets a goal to visit a place and then all the pieces fall into place for her trips.

Keeping travel files of my own has frequently enhanced my trips as well. A business-trip to New Orleans turned into a sightseeing bonanza because of my travel file folder on the city. Before the trip, I created an itinerary. During our stay we referred to the itinerary and dined at great restaurants, visited quaint shops that were tucked away in the city, and went on an outstanding historical tour. I was familiar with all of the city's highlights, and was periodically an experienced native due to my reading at home. Working on your travel files prepares you for an opportunity that doesn't exist yet, but believe me preparation isn't lost time. Due to your diligence, many of your dreams will come to pass sooner than you think.

### Keep a Travel Journal

As your travel dreams come true, the travel journal is an essential tool to document the wonders of your experiences. Journalizing is an extremely effective technique to pull together your thoughts and ideas. It improves your experiences by providing an accurate account of your memories. My travel journal is so interesting to read through and look at. Is has almost become a picture book due to my habit of taking several photos of anything that stands out to me. The photos pages are great because I can paste my photo on the journal page and then write my text next to it.

I usually save any items that contribute to the memory of the event to decorate my pages. My travel journal has ticket stubs, receipts from a special purchase, and even ribbon glued in from a special gift I received while traveling. Throughout the travel journal, I designated a place to record great restaurants and hotels. These sections are filled with special notations about the owners of establishments we visited, the best time to dine at certain restaurants, what the bathrooms looked like, etc. I also keep a log of the names of each hotel's concierge, notes on how the service was, and much more. By using your own travel journal, you will be accumulating valuable information thereby enhancing the quality of future trips.

**Travel Scrap Book**

This is much like the travel journal but not as intimate. This is more of a coffee table book, for everyone to see. It shouldn't contain your secret thoughts, your discoveries or your breakthrough ideas. Instead, pack it with photos, and small captions that highlight your trip. There is a great variety of sticker paper and frames available today for scrapbooking your memories. With a little effort, your scrapbook can blossom into an outstanding documentary of your travels.

**Never leave home without a camera**

This is a travel catastrophe. Some things can never be recounted, some things can never be described, some things can never be retold, and some things can never be understood, without the power of pictures. Take a snapshot of every moment you can, for some things in life, are gone in a flash.

**Travel Tips for** *Convenience*

- Tag your bags before you get to the airport. Buy yourself some unique travel tags that will stand out so you can find your luggage easily.
- On the airplane, bring your own magazines or book to read, unless you have business to work on.
- Tote a small bottle of water with you.

- Travel with your address book or just take an index card with the addresses of people you'll want to send postcards to. You can also create a file on your smart phone.
- Invest in durable luggage that won't come unzipped or rip easily.
- If you plan to buy new things, bring an empty suitcase or duffle bag to fill.
- When you arrive at your destination, brighten your hotel room with fresh flowers and spray the beds with linen spray.
- Bring stamps from home so it's easy to mail your letters or postcards.

## Travel Tips for Safety

- Bring a flashlight with you if you'll be walking to a rental car in a dimmed parking garage. You can get one that hangs on your key chain.
- Use luggage tags with a flap or zipper to conceal your name and address from strangers. It's better to use your work address on your luggage tag for safety.
- Don't announce your credit card number out loud. Either show the card or write down the number.

## Hotel Check In:

- Stay alert during your hotel check in and be watchful of who is around you.
- Park your rental car in a well-lit area close to the entry door.
- When you register, use your first initial and last name only.
- Change rooms if the hotel clerk announces your room number aloud. The proper procedure is to write down the guest's room number on a card that holds the room key.
- If a bellman is helping you get luggage and packages from your car, don't walk away. Make sure everything is on the cart before leaving his presence. I've had bags left behind on a few occasions.

## How to Tip while Traveling

- Airport curbside check in: $1+ per bag
- Hotel Bellman: $2-$5. Tip on the higher end if they inform you of amenities, offer restaurant information, or get the ice for you. The more expensive the hotel, the higher the expected tip.
- Valet Parking: $2-$4 is good

- Concierge tipping varies depending on the quality of service provided. My husband has tipped between $10-$20 for delivering flowers or getting us tickets to a sold out Broadway show. He tips even more if they get dinner reservations at an exclusive establishment.
- Now you have the travel tips you need to be a savvy while on the go. Be encouraged to get out and do more. New experiences lead to new inspiration and new opportunities.

## On Your Return

No matter how beautiful or exciting my destination, the comfort and joys of home are always missed. Make arrangements to return home to an inviting atmosphere. Start early and be organized when packing for your trip, so you aren't forced to return to a house in disarray. Make plans for your own arrival. What will you do after your return home? Will you greet your children, call your mother, or drink a cup of tea? Whatever your choice, do it consistently and make it a gratifying addition to your travel routine. A peaceful entry into your own pleasant surroundings is the perfect way to end any trip.

# CREATE a COLLAGE

## Designing My Life to Enjoy
## Travel

Use the layout on the following page to design your vision in this area. Get glue sticks, magazines and cut out words and pictures to create an Enjoy Life Collage.

Is there a destination that you've been looking to go? Do you see yourself as a world traveler? Imagine how a luxury hotel would give you a creative surge. Would you like to take a cruise around the world? Create a page that describes your globetrotting preferences.

Designing a Life to Enjoy
# CREATE A COLLAGE
LifeCoach2Women.com

# CHAPTER 8

# Enjoy

*Paper*

*"The touch and feel of uncommonly beautiful paper says more about you than you ever could."*
*–attributed to Crane's Paper Company*

Paper has a variety of uses. It impacts every facet of our lives. In this technology era where emails and text messages reign, writing a letter is a more personal way in which we express ourselves in print. From wrapping gifts of love to printing newspapers and magazines to the fine stationery on which we write our most intimate messages, paper is still a way we communicate worldwide.

As with fashion, the type of paper that you use to communicate with is a direct indication of your style, status, and state of mind. My first encounter with grand paper was when I was in a New York stationery store called *Paper Affair*.

The small sheets of wrapping paper that lined the back wall looked like ice cream flavors to me. I selected several prints in a variety of colors and textures: embossed, geometric shapes, and fashionable prints. At the conclusion of my jaunt through the store, I headed to the sales counter with glee. "What great paper finds!" I thought. When the sales lady gave me my total, I instantly realized that this was another level of paper purchasing for me. Despite the considerable investment, I was thrilled by the presentations that I would be able to make with these exquisite papers. I knew then, that I had discovered another element of my personal style.

*"You don't really know a woman until you have had a letter from her."*
*—Ada Leverson*

## Stationery

Your choice of writing paper conveys an important message. The color, texture, and font types on your stationery all speak volumes about how you wish to present yourself to the world. A letter you send involves much more than the words written. The paper, writing instrument, and presentation all come together to make your message complete. So, if you have neglected to enhance your life with personal stationery, put it on your to do list. Take an hour or so for a paper excursion and visit the finest paper store in your area. While browsing through your local paperie, select a paper and envelope to have personalized, so you're prepared to write a formal letter at any time.

Your stationery wardrobe should be customized to fit a variety of social occasions. Envelopes are as important as the paper, so select them carefully. I have formal stationery with matching envelopes, but I find it more fun to collect several different types of witty papers and stationery cards. Stunning stationery makes a lasting impression. The reader may save your letter and read it again long after it's been sent. Even if they are reading your letter years later for the 100th time, you want them to admire the paper and recall your personal sense of style.

Unique stationery stores exist all over the world. Therefore, wherever my travels lead me, I try to visit one of the local stationery boutiques. On many occasions I've stopped into quaint little stationery stores and left with bags full of new stationery cards, notebooks and journals. Once while shopping, my eye fell on a card that shouted "Stacia" all over it. The paper was orange and fuchsia. Ahh, love at first sight. So, of course I purchased several packets of the lovely raspberry and creamsicle hued stationery and went on my merry way.

Invest in the stationery that fits you best. It can be playful or serious, traditional, romantic, or strikingly colorful. Whatever it is you are trying to communicate, you can find the paper and envelopes to match your mood.

## Wrapping Paper

Today there are hundreds of styles of wrapping paper. We can venture out and try new textures and shades. The presentation of a gift is just as important as the gift itself. There is such delight when we are presented with a beautifully wrapped gift. You almost hesitate to open it, so you just bask in the glory of the wrapping. One year for Christmas, one of my assistants presented me with several boxes wrapped in the most beautiful pink paper, showcased in a thick black and white polka dot ribbon that was tied in luxurious bows. The packaging was breathtaking. Of course, the gift was nice too, but I've never forgotten the careful thought and effort that must have gone into wrapping that gift so I would absolutely love it.

While visiting an art supply store, I purchased some purple paper for a special person that would make the same impact when I presented their gift. Now in order to keep your wrapping paper looking good as new, you must store the rolls. I keep my rolls in plastic storage containers.

### Personalized Gift Tags and Labels

With minimal computer skills, you can create your own personal designs, gifts, and labels yourself. Just recently, I had some gift tags and labels designed and printed for myself that reflect my certain kind of chic. One label has a pair of green and fuchsia shoes with my name on it. The other displays a fuchsia and yellow handbag with my name on it. I use them on gifts, folders, and even as a letter seal at times. Your gift tags will add a signature touch to your presents.

### Colored Paper Files

To add purpose and meaning to your life, keep Purpose Files. Choose 5-7 categories of interest to you. Label file folders with those categories, and begin to clip, sort, collect, and save information that fit into your sections. To enhance your Purpose Files, find unique shaped folders, portfolio cases, or standard file folders in bright colors and trendy textures.

### Invitations

One of my favorite hobbies is to hunt for and stock up on beautiful blank invitations papers. Your invitations set the tone for your upcoming celebration. It's another way I prepare for an opportunity that doesn't exist yet. After I purchase the invitations, I look for the perfect way to fill in the blanks.

For instance, I found this pink-striped vellum invites with fashion silhouettes dancing around the border of the paper. The far edges were trimmed in gold foil. Immediately, I purchased 10 blank invitations. A few weeks later, someone asked me if I was interested in attending a grand fashion show...Voila! The invitations instantly came to mind. "I'll take nine tickets," I said. Needless to say, the invitations were used to invite my guests to a fabulous night of fashion.

A similar scenario describes how one of my favorite tea parties came about. The invitations had been sitting in my tea party invitation box for several months. One day while looking through the box for some ideas, it dawned on me that it was time to meet with all the wives of all the men who worked in leadership for my husband. My theme for the tea party was Tea & Intimacy. My goal was to encourage the leaders to continue relating to their husbands with intimacy and among each other as good friends. To coincide with the theme on the invitations, the gifts were intimate apparel, lingerie laundry wash, and a lingerie bag for their intimate apparel. The ladies also received fabulous gift baskets filled with stationery, lovely pens with assorted ink colors, and other lovely items that fit with the theme.

## Paper Collage

Displayed in the center of the wall in my office is my Creativity Board, which is a corkboard that I have personalized by decorating it with my signature colors. Coordinating it with the seasons in my life, this board speaks to my works in progress. It's filled with paper, some printed invitations of past or upcoming events, blank pages which need to be filled with catchy phrases and beautiful ribbons that I love, but haven't found a reason to use. Clippings from magazines can also be found on my creativity board. This collage of materials is really a collection of my thoughts and the beginning of many divine ideas. Once I complete the season that my paper collage represents, I clear my board, file, or discard my papers, and begin with a blank canvas. My designers approach to working on projects has rubbed off on my staff because all of the ladies have created boards in their offices as well. You can often walk through our office and see one of our employees that is working on a new project, just gazing at their board as if it were the Mona Lisa. What they are actually doing is drawing inspiration from their paper collection of ideas.

## Paper Stores

If you are looking for ideas to spice up your invitations or add flavor to your paper work, visiting a paper store could do the trick. You can make personalized calendars, gift tags, calling cards, even custom posters. I love visiting paper stores, from stationery to journals there is so much creativity to enjoy. Seeing all the colored sheets stacked on their shelves, all of the stylish journals each with their own flare and all kinds of notepads too. When adding the extra expense printing, please note that the proper paper choice can upgrade any presentation.

Create your next agenda or make your to do list on colored paper. Put together a colorful book report folder for yourself or your kids, using assorted colored paper. Making use of the expertise at your local print shop will certainly raise the level of excellence for your paper presentations.

We all use paper to communicate, but not everyone uses paper to make a statement. Now that you've been enlightened, make an impression whenever you have something to say. Whether by color or texture, design or weight, utilize the power of pretty paper to speak highly of you and make your communication more pleasurable.

# CREATE A COLLAGE

Designing My Life to Enjoy:

## Paper

**Use the layout on the following page to design your vision in this area. Get glue sticks, magazines and cut out words and pictures to create an Enjoy Life Collage.**

How do you want to be perceived when someone receives mail from you? Would your stationery style be fun or more conservative? What type of wrapping paper suits your taste? Do you dream of having a wrapping center? Make a collage that describes your pretty paper fantasies.

Designing a Life to Enjoy
# CREATE A COLLAGE
LifeCoach2Women.com

# CHAPTER 9
# Enjoy
## Letter Writing

*"We have never talked together the way we have sometimes in letter.*
*Why do I meet people better in letters?"*
*– Anne Morrow Lindbergh*

I just couldn't discuss my love of paper without sharing with you the art of letter writing. For centuries letter writing has been a premium form of communication. From the most passionate love letters to the most detailed plans of war, letter writing creates a close bond that even great distances cannot destroy. Though all the world may turn to E-Mail Euphoria, knowing that "You've Got Mail" is still more gratifying when it comes to you in the form of a letter. The art of letter writing is a life enhancer. A letter gives us time to reflect and share what's on our hearts more clearly and completely. Letter writing should be a routine part of your enjoyable life, just like lunching with other ladies or taking a tea break. As with any art, there are ways to develop your letter writing expertise. The more practice the better. The following information will provide you with an easy guideline for writing memorable letters.

### Be Prepared

Continue to develop your stationery wardrobe, so that it includes an assortment of paper styles. Keep fun personalized stationery in a handy spot. I use a bright yellow box to house the favorites of my collection. Treat yourself to colorful or decorated paper that complements your personality and makes letter writing more exciting. Keep your stamp and envelopes handy. Purchase return address labels. Collect cards for all occasions and keep them on hand. Every time you send a card, make the extra effort to personalize it with a written note of your own thoughts.

Purchase special writing pens. The instrument you write with should be a pleasure to use. Here are some of my favorites:

/ **The Sensa**
/ **Cross Pens**
/ **Mont Blanc**

- **Poppin' Pens**
- **Gel Pens** – I know they don't quite compare on the quality scale, but they're still one of my favorites because they make my creativity surge.

## Set Aside Time

Schedule a letter-writing day. My daughter and I have one day a month that we use to write personal letters for about an hour. We look forward to sharing what's going on in our lives during this time. I realize that you won't have an entire day to pen an artful letter every time you need to drop someone a line. Yet, taking advantage of the little snippets of opportunity during the day will help you make time to stay in touch.

*Take advantage of waiting time. Make use of pauses in your day like sitting in the doctor or dentist's office. Keep a petite package of stationery with you that fits neatly in your purse for such occasions.

*Make a list of people you want to write to. Don't let a swamped schedule be your excuse. The busiest (and most successful) people always find time to communicate with those people in their network.

## Stay Focused

Write as though you were sitting across the table from the person to which you are writing. Share what you would say to them in person. Keep the same train of thought throughout your letter so that it is not tedious to read. Don't worry about conforming to any set of rules for letter writing. Be yourself. Heartfelt sharing is what letter writing is all about.

## Develop Your Style

I try to write all of my letters so that they energize, inspire, and spark ideas for the readers. I write to motivate and stimulate. What is your style? Are you a romantic? Do you enjoy writing poetry or are you a comedian at heart? Whatever your fancy, use your style to amuse and encourage the reader.

## Be Inquisitive

By asking questions you will give the person on the receiving end of your letter an interesting starting point to write you back. Make your question specific. Ask the "W" questions: who, what, where, when and why.

## Be Appropriate

When I am writing letters to my mentors, I usually thank them for their impartation and tell them how their information has helped me. I don't expect them to write back. I choose my words very carefully when writing a business letter, or a letter to the masses. You don't want to be interpreted the wrong way. Reread your letters before you send them. Ask yourself, "Does this make sense? Is this letter offensive in any way?" Get a co-worker or friend or proof read your letter if possible.

### Collect Information

The next time you come across an amusing cartoon, see an interesting article in a magazine, newspaper clipping, or read a good book, save them in your files. If it applies to something a friend or a colleague enjoys, send it to them. They will appreciate your thoughtfulness. Never throw away a good letter. The written words of others become very precious as the years go by.

### End on a Positive Note

Even if you must discuss some weighty issues, don't compose a depressing, faithless letter. Send letters of hope, faith, and encouragement and your readers will always welcome your correspondence. Date your letter with the day, month, and year. This will help when you are trying to refer back to a certain time period in your life.

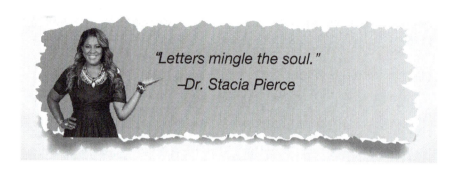

*"Letters mingle the soul."*
–Dr. Stacia Pierce

## The Benefits of Letter Writing

- It helps you develop your writing style.
- Your connection is more intimate between you and the correspondent.
- You can fill someone's day with joy.

# 10 Fun Ways to Drop Someone a Line

✉ 1. Put letters in your children's lunch box telling them how great they are.

✉ 2. Mail a love letter to your husband at his office.

✉ 3. Make a list of all the great attributes of one of your friends and mail it to them.

✉ 4. Write a note inside each book that you give away as a present.

✉ 5. Leave a note of appreciation attached to the refrigerator to pleasantly surprise your home caregiver.

✉ 6. If you're a company owner or supervisor, send a motivational memo to your workers that both inspires and challenges them to accomplish more.

✉ 7. If there are mentors who have been exceedingly supportive of you, send them a note of thanks.

✉ 8. Send a card or letter to your parents or mentor to let them know how much you appreciate them.

9. **Attach a beautiful card to a flower arrangement and send it to a friend who's ill.**

10. **For a friend who's in transition, mail them a letter attached to a clean baby diaper. On the outside of the envelope, write, "At some point in life, we all need a change".**

These are just a few ideas, but be creative in sending your letters to your associates, friends, and family. Don't forget to pick beautiful papers that you would treasure even with out the words. When you send your letters attached to gifts, be sure that the gift is wrapped to express your personal style. Wrap even the simplest gifts with love and flair and your kind gesture will be treasured for a long time.

# CREATE A COLLAGE

Designing My Life to Enjoy:

## Letter Writing

**Use the layout on the following page to design your vision in this area. Get glue sticks, magazines and cut out words and pictures to create an Enjoy Life Collage.**

What is your writing style? What type of pens would fit your personal style? Would you enjoy writing with various types of ink? Although letter writing can be considered a lost art, imagine how your friends and family feel after reading one of your letters. Create a collage that explains your letter writing loves.

*Designing a Life to Enjoy*

# CREATE A COLLAGE

LifeCoach2Women.com

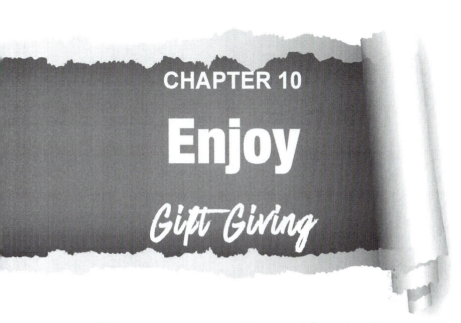

# CHAPTER 10

# Enjoy

## Gift Giving

*"No person was ever honored for what he received. Honor is the reward of what one gives."*
*–Calvin Coolidge*

Gift giving spreads joy and uplifts the human spirit. Making a heartfelt effort to offer someone a present that is in touch with their preferences and passions is a gift that reaches far beyond material value. A gift communicates your love and appreciation for those to whom you give. Becoming highly skilled at gift giving will endow you with a knack to bring cheer into the lives of those who surround you. Enjoy Gift Giving speaks to those who want to increase their ability to share their blessings and bestow a bit of happiness.

Have you ever been so excited about giving a gift that you could hardly wait for them to open it? Did you find yourself perched over their shoulder with a grin as big as Texas waiting for them to unwrap the gift that showed how much you really cared? That is the joy of gift giving. Without these life experiences, your life is void of feelings of pure gratification that you can't get from any other source. Whether or not you have experienced the gift-giving rush, get ready for a real adventure. By the time you reach the gift giving resource page, you will have transformed into a gift-giving guru.

If you're like me, you have had those days where you needed to purchase a gift and had no clue what to get. Don't be ashamed, it's happened to us all, but I have figured out a way that you can avoid gift-giving woes forever. My fail-proof gift-giving guide will help you make the best gift choices every time.

## Organizing Your Gift Giving

### Create a List

Creating a gift list will give you a plan when you're planning for Christmas, a birthday, bridal shower, or any other special occasion that requires gifts. Onto your list write down the names of all the people you plan to buy for. As the opportunity presents itself, gather information from them that will make your gift finder easier. If budgeting is a concern, put how much you are willing to spend next to each name and total your gift purchasing account. Now you have a realistic picture of the maximum amount you may be spending.

## Create a Budget for Giving

Set aside a certain amount of money each month just for the sake of giving. You could even open a savings account. For Christmas, most banks have a Christmas Club Savings Plan where you can put money into the account without access to it until the holidays.

## Keep Gift Slips

For every person that is a VIP in my network, I have gift file cards that I keep on them. I made these cards on a heavy cardstock so that they file away easily. Then, they are color coded by categories: boss/mentor, leaders/staff, family/relatives, friends/business associates etc. On the back of each slip there is a ledger to keep track of what I have given of each person and when. Once you create your slips, group them first by color. Next, arrange them alphabetically by last name. Purchase a beautiful stationery box or index card box to store all of your slips.

## Keep a Gift Giving File

Get a pretty colored file folder and label it "Gift Giving". Now throughout the year, whenever you are looking in a magazine or online and see something that would be a great gift for someone on your list, file the information in your folder. During a routine shopping trip or your travels, when you see an item you plan to purchase at a later date, write down all the information. Note the store you're in, the name of the item, the price, the style number, and the barcode information. Be sure to jot down the person for whom you planned to purchase the gift. Put that information in your file when you return home.

---

*Gift Giving Card*

Name: _____     Store: _____

Address:_____     Item(s):_____

Phone # _____     Price: _____

Suit Size: _____     Notes: _____

Shoe Size: _____     _____

Dress Size: _____

Favorite designers: _____

_____

Favorite colors: _____

_____

---

# 8 Keys to Gracious Gift Giving

*"The manner of giving is worth more than the gift."*

*—Pierre Corneille*

### Develop Your Gift-Giving Style

Your style sets you apart from everyone else. Define your style of giving. Are you known for using a certain color pen? Are gift baskets your way of creatively giving? Have gifts that are unique, one-of-a-kind finds that become your signature. I use personalized gift tags and labels to stamp my signature style on each gift I give. The tags I choose display my personal style, they are fashionably whimsy and colorful. Whatever you give should carry an air of you.

### Wrap Your Gifts with Flair

Presentation is as important as the gift itself. Go on the hunt for unique papers and ribbons. At times, try to use unconventional techniques for wrapping. For example, use a unique box or you could fill a wagon with toys for your favorite child. To cater to a gardener, you could fill a flowerpot with gardening tools.

## Give What You Would Like to Receive

Do for others what you would want done for you. Think of how you would like to be honored; then extend that gift to someone else.

## Give Accurately

Sometimes it's best to simply give someone what they want and have asked for. There is nothing more fulfilling than getting a dream come true. A couple of times, my staff has asked me for a dream gift list and purchased me everything on it! I was extremely surprised and very satisfied. Generic gifts never provide a WOW experience. Always make your best effort to present a gift that is sensational.

## Give Gifts That Expand People

Giving a person a mind-expanding experience is very rewarding. On occasion I like to give gift certificates to unique stores that the recipient wouldn't normally shop at. Chosen thoughtfully, books can also be mind-expanding gifts. It is always a joy to heighten someone's awareness of the arts by giving them tickets to a cultural event.

Nearly every holiday, I discover a new book that is perfect for gift giving to my family and friends. Information can change the seasons of someone's life. Just the right book at the properly appointed time can illuminate a person's purpose in life.

> "One's life has value so long as one attributes value to the life of others, by means of love, friendship, indignation and compassion."
> –Simone De Beauvoir

### Give Big When You Can

Often when it comes time to shower someone with gifts if we analyze the person and decide they already have enough, we tend to scale back on our gift. I make special effort to do the exact opposite. When someone is well to do, I make an even greater effort to bless them with more than they expect. If it is a person of honor, I think it's important to honor them with a gift on their level. I don't ever try to downscale my gift when I'm giving to someone great. I strive to give something memorable and impactful. I never want my gift to be the one that they don't remember I like to make a lasting impression.

## Give Surprise Packages of Joy

Surprise packages of joy are gifts that aren't given for a special occasion. Don't restrict yourself to presenting gifts only on birthdays, anniversaries, or the holidays. It is so much fun to give and receive unexpected presents. Whenever I'm out and find something that matches the tastes or purpose of one of my closest friends, I purchase it. I always have it gift wrapped, and cheerfully send it, knowing that my friends will gleefully open the package and realize that I was thinking of them.

I give things to people daily. Whether it's food, clothes, or just because gifts, I enjoy blessing others. Whenever an opportunity comes up to give more than I've ever given, I step up to the challenge. Recently at my birthday party, although I was the person being celebrated, I surprised each of my guests with a book or two that suited their personality as well as an article of clothing. Every person in attendance went home with a goody bag as well. It was my way of showing how much I appreciate my friends and family. I planned the event for months and took time to think of just the right item for each person. My thoughtfulness made a big impact and weeks later people were still coming up to me with heartfelt words of appreciation.

**Surprise Treasure Tips**

*If you ever host a seminar or conference, a nice touch for your guest speakers is to add special gifts in their hotel room.*

*For overnight guests in your home place a special treasure on their nightstand or bed. Welcoming your guests with gifts always causes them to enjoy their stay a little bit more.*

**Create A Gift Closet**

To be prepared for special occasions, gather up goodies to put in your gift closet. I look for bargains after Christmas and at the end of summer for items to stock in my closet. For young children: board games, matchbox cars, Barbie dolls, Legos, and videos games are all appropriate gifts for birthday parties and Christmas presents. Towels, books, journals, photo albums, men's shaving kits, perfumes, and colognes are all excellent gifts for adults. Keep wrapping paper, gift cards, ribbons, scotch tape, shopping bags, a few boxes, and colored tissue on hand for the proper presentation. It's much easier to give spontaneously when you are well supplied. Maintaining a gift closet will help you stay organized and prepared for any gift-giving adventure.

**Here Are Some Secrets to Fantastic Finds**

1. Make gift buying a year round process.

2. Review the calendar a month or two in advance so you're aware of upcoming gift giving occasions.

3. When out of town or on vacation, it's the perfect time to gift shop. Often, different regions carry unique gifts one cannot easily find.

4. Shop odd shops and specialty stores for one-of-a-kind presents.

5. Listen for clues. Often a boss, mentor, or friend will reveal what they are currently working on or need during a conversation that will direct you to the perfect gift.

6. If you spot a great gift, GET IT (even if you don't know exactly who it's for)! Generally, you'll never see the same thing again and you'll wish you had purchased it.

7. Don't forget to keep your gift-wrapping supplies well stocked at your house so you can immediately wrap the gifts you purchased.

8. When filling your gift closet, purchase an assortment of general gifts (stationery, tea cups,

journals, books, bath and body products, etc.) for last minute occasions.

9. Purchase a gift on-line. Often they can send it wrapped directly to the recipient.

10. Give "shopping free" gifts such as a gift certificate to a spa, tickets to a play, a magazine subscription, a dinner for two gift certificate, etc.

# CREATE A COLLAGE

Designing My Life to Enjoy:

## Gift Giving

**Use the layout on the following page to design your vision in this area. Get glue sticks, magazines and cut out words and pictures to create an Enjoy Life Collage.**

Think about those closest to you. What types of gifts would you like to give them? What will be your gift giving signature? How can you give more to your mentors and leaders? Create a page that displays your gift giving style.

Designing a Life to Enjoy
# CREATE A COLLAGE
LifeCoach2Women.com

# CHAPTER 11

# Enjoy

## *Flowers*

*"More than anything I must have flowers. Always, always."*
*– Claude Monet*

Surrounding yourself with splendid colors, aromatic fragrances, unchallenged beauty, and feelings of peace and well-being can be easily accomplished by bringing fresh flowers on the scene. Flowers are such a simple way to add luxury to your environment. If you've ever been given flowers, you can grasp those memories in an instant, due to the lasting impression the gift of flowers leaves. At pivotal moments in my life, the sight and smell of flowers had a great impact on my future. For nearly six months into the beginning of our courtship, my husband sent flower arrangement sealed with a motivational note each week. This experience sparked a love for fresh flowers and my husband that will last forever.

Whether placed discreetly on the counter or in the center of an elaborate dinner table, the right floral arrangement will set the stage and create the mood for an inspired gathering. Flowers help us to enjoy life; we use them to celebrate, to send a message of love (like my husband did), or simply to brighten our days. Add to the loveliness of your life-style by making flowers a part of your daily surroundings. Fresh flowers are so important to me that I added their cost to our weekly grocery budget. The whole experience of choosing just the right flowers to come home to and arrange in a lovely vase, is in itself, enjoyable.

Having the right vase to enhance our décor is important. Begin to hunt for a variety of vases that appeal to you. Subtly place your flowers throughout your home in intimate places. Catching a glimpse of your favorite vases filled with beautiful arrangements, is sure to trigger a joyful smile as you go about your day. You can find vases with extensive detail for nominal amounts. A friend of mine finds her vases while antiquing on Saturday mornings. I, on the other hand, enjoy modern, art deco style vases, so I usually acquire them during my travels in quaint little shops throughout America.

Adding flowers to your décor can instantly change the ambience or atmosphere of a room. You deserve to have little beauty treats in your décor that give you a daily lift and that's what flowers do. Sigmund Freud said: "Flowers are restful to look at they have neither emotions nor conflicts." Spending two to three days in a hotel room several times a month can be disheartening, but I change the scenery by creating a peaceful, homelike atmosphere with fresh flowers.

Soon after arrival, their floral fragrance fills the room bringing a familiarity and just for a moment, I am able to forget that I am in a lifeless hotel room and feel as if I were home. If the weather and my schedule permits, I purchase flowers at a nearby market and have them delivered. Periodically, I am pleasantly surprised by the delivery of a gorgeous bouquet from my husband. However the flowers arrive, they are more than welcome. During times of retreat and reflection, pamper yourself with flowers. Adorn your breakfast tray or vanity with a small bouquet of flowers to add beauty and personal pleasure to your mornings. Just as flowers comforted me away from home, they can warmly greet your guests. The next time you have house guests, decorate their room with flowers for an extra touch of hospitality.

> *"No occupation is so delightful to me as the culture of the earth and no culture comparable to that of the garden."*
> *— Thomas Jefferson*

### The Flower Garden

Whatever your decorating style, start a floral custom today. Decide which fresh flowers are your favorites and plant them in your yard. If the thought of you gardening is laughable, hire someone, or ask a friend who has a green thumb to help. I don't currently have a garden, nor do I practice gardening, but I was forever touched when I toured Eleanor and Edsel Ford's mansion in Grosse Point, MI. We strolled through the rose garden and as the breeze carried the aroma of fresh flowers across our path it caused my adrenaline to soar. As the tour continued, I became more excited as the guide explained how each day during the spring and summer months, fresh flowers were cut and arranged in several vases and then placed all over the entire house.

As our guide narrated the story of the Ford's life-style, I knew I would one day have a rose garden and gardener to tend to it as well. I captured my thoughts on paper immediately after returning home.

Have you thought about beautifying the exterior of your house with flowers? Or dreamed of having an awe striking landscape to spruce up the curb appeal of your home? Your yard and entrance create a mood, so create one that will be uplifting when you pull up to your home.

One thing I do, as seasons change, I place big beautiful wreaths on my front door and place a welcome mat right beneath it. Try standing in front of your home (even if you live in an apartment, town house or condominium) and ask what message is the entryway sending? What can you do about it to make it better? Flowers can be a simple way of adding elegant character to that entrance which introduces people to your household.

### Sending Flowers

Knowing the power flowers have to light up our lives, I try to send them to friends and family at unexpected times. Did you know that flowers have more "cheer power" than most other gifts? According to a study at Rutgers University, flowers gain a greater response in cheering up the recipients than other gifts. The university sent researchers trained to recognize facial expressions to the homes of 147 women and noted their reactions as they received various gifts.

Each of the three gifts: a candle and holder, a fruit basket, and a flower arrangement were all worth $50. Yet, researchers found the gift of fresh flowers proved to be more appreciated. According to researchers, 100 percent of the women who got flowers exhibited a broad, excited smile associated with genuine happiness. On the other hand, only 8 percent of fruit recipients and 13 percent of those who received candles gave polite grins which lacked true happiness.

The psychologist noted that those who received flowers proceeded to socialize more, and reported a greater overall emotional boost. Traditionally, we send flowers when there has been a loss in someone's life to show our concern. Be that as it may, based on these findings, the receiver doesn't really get the opportunity to enjoy the flowers because they are distressed and focused elsewhere. So, in addition to traditional occasions, sends flowers when you want a person's day to be exceptional.

I have also sent flowers as a thank you to conference hosts: authors: retail store sales ladies: and concierges who have helped me significantly. This practice has caused numerous people, from all walks of life, to look upon me favorably.

Never send flowers haphazardly; do your homework. Find out if the receiver has a particular flower they are fond of. Are they allergic to any flowers? What is their color preference? Do they adore large or small bouquets and what type of vase will tickle their fancy?

For example, I'm fond of topiaries; so much so that after having fresh ones made for one of my events, I had them duplicated in silk. The four topiaries are now beautifully displayed in my home. Everyone has preferences. If you investigate, you can make sure your gift is well received. Whenever I send flowers, I ask my florist to create something that will fit the receiver's personal taste and style.

When I'm planning an event, I assist my florist by informing them of my theme and colors so they can coordinate the floral arrangements with the general décor. I love my florist, they know my style. I've been working with them for several years now. Whenever you are planning an event take an extra pinch of care when choosing a florist and the décor is sure to come out fabulous.

## How to Choose a *Florist*

Word of mouth. A good recommendation often helps save time and money in the long run. Asking your friends or family if they know a good florist is normally a good idea because those close to you are most familiar with your taste. They are more likely to recommend someone whose style you will adorn. If using a conference center or rented facility, ask for the name of a florist who has previously decorated that location successfully.

## *Dig* for Information

Deciding the overall look you want for an entire event is top priority. This will help you ask the right questions when visiting the floral shop. Don't be too shy to ask questions and compare prices. Note the different style, prices, plans, etc. of each florist.

## On the *Money*

Make a budget indicating how much you are willing to spend for your arrangements, and ask each florist what you can expect for that amount. It is possible that estimates will greatly vary. Some florists include the transportation costs and additional charges for wire and ribbon. Others will just quote the flower costs so be sure you are clear on what the estimates include.

## Your *Friend* the Florist

It is really important that you develop a good working relationship with your florist. Be sure that they understand exactly what you want as well as what you like. Keep checking back with them; especially the person you will be working with on the big day.

## The *Floral* Front

The actual florist shop is a great indicator of the skills and creativity of the employees. Keep your eyes open for a large variety of fresh flowers and innovative presentations when visiting your local floral shop.

## Picture *Perfect*

Don't make your final decision on a florist until you see their portfolio. Premiere florists should be able to show you pictures showcasing events using different styles, color themes and arrangements. This could be in person or online.

## *It's* a Date!

As soon as you can, book the florist you like best. Booking three to four months ahead of time is usually the advance notice that is requested. Get everything, including the date of the event, the cost, and any other necessary details in writing. At this point, a small deposit (20% of the total cost) is normally required.

## Problem Free *Planning*

Steer clear of trouble by equipping your florist with as many details as you can. Give them sketches of fabric swatches from surrounding furniture or table linen, color swatches from the other decorations, pictures, or magazine pages of arrangements that you like and so on. Bring your florist whatever information you can to prevent misunderstanding and make sure the floral presentation is just what you want. Touch base with them about two weeks before your event. The florist should be able to show you a combination of the flowers that you previously selected. Be sure to confirm the delivery times at this meeting.

## The Power of *Flowers*

Flowers around the house just seem to add rich simplicity. Even the simplest bouquet can transform any room in your home. When flowers are missing from around my house it seems like the décor is incomplete. My whole family has grown accustomed to their presence.

# Designer *Bouquet*

It can be very expensive to purchase flowers from a floral designer, which is basically an upscale florist (it's like upgrading from a mall department store to an exclusive boutique). However, I do splurge on occasion for very special events. If you, on the other hand, have a natural bent towards creating arrangements, take the "floral challenge" like several of my very savvy friends have done. One enrolled in a floral design course to learn professional techniques for arranging her own flowers. Now she is developing a lovely style of her own.

I purchased a few books on flower designing and keep a file folder on centerpieces, arranging, and flower decorating how to's. Although I'm learning little tricks of the trade, it is not a passion of mine, nor do I want to spend a lot of time pursuing the how to's of beautiful arrangements. Instead, I just added to my dream list all of the floral designers who one day will decorate a grand event for me. The phenomenal floral designer Anthony Todd whose bouquets can be frequently spotted at Manhattan's DKNY store is first on my list. In the meantime, I can share a few tricks of the trade with you to help make your floral arrangement look smashing, just in case Mr. Todd isn't able to assist you quite yet.

# You Can Do It!
## At-Home Floral Techniques

 Use a monochromatic palette with one type of flower for a contemporary look. You could start with the faintest lavender rose to a medium purple to the deepest violet.

 To create a beautiful swirl of stems with a flawless alignment, New York florist Michael George gives this advice: Carefully line up and twist the stems, twist slightly and secure with a clear rubber band which are sold at cosmetics stores.

 Remember that bigger is not necessarily better when it comes to choosing your vase. If you want an arrangement that looks lush it is easier and less expensive to use a smaller vase.

 With a little flair, you can use whatever containers you like. Even a plain drinking glasses can be turned into a stylish vase. Select a mix of tumblers and other glasses to arrange with a small cluster of flowers in each. Whether on the counter top or tabletop, this technique makes for a very elegant look.

Whatever the technique you choose to use be sure that it is woven into your personal style. Choosing your favorite floral decor to create an eye-filling environment in each room is a fine way to entice your family and guests to enjoy a pleasant, personal air of you whenever they enter your home.

Start where you are if you aren't ready to hire a florist or begin to design your own bouquet, simply stroll and buy from the wondrous aisle of your local grocery store. There you can find a bouquet of beauty that's perfect for you. Cruise the flower department (in most stores they are located near the entrance). Look for deals and check out the colors, it's like having your own personal garden at your fingertips.

### *Flower* To Do's:

- Create a list of people you would like to send flowers to as a thank you.

- Make a flower log. To keep you prepared to send flowers in an instant, write down your closest friend, their favorite flowers, and colors.

- Discover what kind of flowers you like and write them down.

- Write a few romantic lines when sending flowers to your sweetheart.

- Send yourself some flowers.

- Practice arranging flowers in a beautiful vase. You may develop a skill that could evolve into a signature style.

- Decorate with flowers for a special gathering.

# CREATE A COLLAGE

Designing My Life to Enjoy:

## Flowers

**Use the layout on the following page to design your vision in this area. Get glue sticks, magazines and cut out words and pictures to create an Enjoy Life Collage.**

Have you always hoped someone would send you a huge bouquet of flowers to show their love for you? Would you like to enroll in a flower arranging class if you had the time? Wouldn't it be lovely to spend a morning strolling through your own personal garden? Create your flower page and fill in your dreams on paper.

Designing a Life to Enjoy
# CREATE A COLLAGE
LifeCoach2Women.com

# CHAPTER 12

# Enjoy

*Fragrance*

*"Perfumes, colors, and sound, echo one another."*
*–Baudelairre*

Fragrance is powerful. It can transport you to distant lands, adjust your state of mind or even assist your body in the healing process. Though sometimes taken for granted, with your sense of smell you can take control of your environment and make your daily living more pleasurable. Whether you are reminded of a charming garden, vacations by the sea, or your favorite meal, fragrances evoke memories and emotions that help us to savor life. Sweet smelling environments are a part of enjoyable living. Scientific studies have discovered that stimulating the brain through perfume can awaken the senses, reduce stress and anxiety, ease depression, alleviate fatigue, and have an uplifting effect. In our quest for overall well being, perfuming yourself and your surroundings has become synonymous with individual style. Fragrance is a joy because there are so many wonderful ways to use it. I use it to perfume m y body, spruce up my beauty time, and enhance my household. Expressing yourself with fragrance infiltrates your surroundings with a personal touch.

## Perfumes that Perk up Your Personality

The fragrance that you wear should be an aromatic witness to who you are and what you prefer. Choosing the right scent to fit your character will perk up your persona and make your presence a savory addition to anyone's day. Aim to build your very own wardrobe of fragrance, but select a favorite to become your signature scent. During this particular process of building my fragrance wardrobe, I created my own line of perfume that suited all of my fragrance needs. I love to have a variety of scents that are my go to when I'm feeling a certain way on some days, and then I like to have my mainstay, my Inspire perfume, that I can put on any time of day and it suits me and the occasion perfectly. Having gone through the manufacturing process it caused me to purge my perfume collection and give many bottles away. I stuck with only the scents that I absolutely love. As a result, in addition to my signature, twelve other wonderful fragrances with a floral base adorn my dressing table. I absolutely love each scent on my vanity and enjoy having the option to decide which perfume I will wear based on that day's agenda and my attitude. To avoid ending up with a tray of perfumes you'll never wear more than once, discover your perfume type.

### Fragrance Categories

Actually, there is no universally recognized system for the thousands of perfumes that exist, though the multitude of Perfumers do agree on a few basic categories: floral oriental, citrus green and even "edible." There are more categories and numerous variations of each, but I've just outlined a simple overview to give you some fragrance family facts. Review the Fragrance Finding chart at the end of this section.

Which category describes your preferred fragrances—Light and citrus-y, fresh and floral, mossy and green, oriental (spicy/musky scents), or edible (which I personally find irresistible)? As your fragrance collection grows, you may decide to choose your fragrance based on a special event you're going to attend or your general mood for that day. Before you get dressed, ponder for a moment how you want your fragrance to make you feel? Sexy, romantic, fresh, energized, calm, youthful, or exotic? Whatever your decision, your fragrance choice should agree.

## When Selecting Your Own Scent

Write down the perfumes you've previously worn and try to group them by types. Flip through magazines and lightly sniff the scent strips of the new fragrances so you can update your knowledge as well as get a feel for your preferences. Tear out those scent strips and carry them around with you in your purse for a few days to see if you really like the fragrance.

## Fragrance Field Trips

Head to the department store perfume department and do your own little study of fragrance. Did you know that midday your sense of smell is sharper? In the past, I've discovered that if I am not intrigued by the name of that fragrance, that the scent won't appeal to me either. Prior to your perfume purchase, pay attention to details like the name, color of the liquid and the bottle design. The bottles of fragrance I choose are usually square or rounder. Your fragrance category should complement your fashion sense. How would you describe your fashion personality? Classic, Romantic, Dramatic, Sporty, or Eccentric? When shopping at the fragrance counter describe your style of dress. If your sales person is a good one, your fashion personality should indicate to them what type of perfume they should recommend to you.

## Fragrance Finding Chart

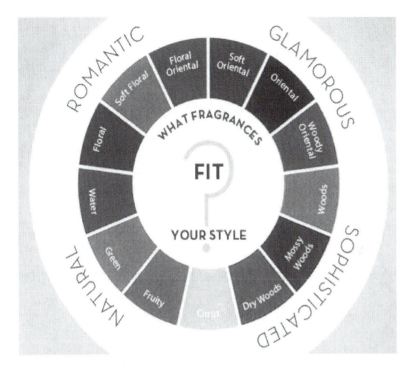

Courtesy of ElizabethArden.com

## Scent and Sensibility

Learn how to properly test fragrances so you don't love any aromatic accidents. When shopping for scents, do not wear a fragrance to the store. Use the paper perfume tester strips to spritz on fragrances. Once you find a perfume you like, test it on your forearm to see how it reacts to your body chemistry. To avoid sensory overload, don't try more than three fragrances at a time. Sniffing coffee beans between each fragrance will clear your head. If you are not sold on the scent at the counter ask for a sample to take home and make your decision later.

### Perfume I.Q. Points

 Perfume should be stored in its box to prolong its potency. If you do not have the box, keep your bottles in a cool, dry place away from sunlight.

 Perfume is sold in different forums, which are categorized by strength of the fragrance. The most concentrated is *perfume*, followed by *eau de parfum*, then *parfum de toilette*, *eau de toilette*, and *eau de cologne*.

 Layering perfume makes the fragrance last longer. To layer, use the shower gel and the lotion that accompanies that scent.

 Combining fragrances gives you a scent that is distinctly your own. I often combine two different perfumes, or interchange their body products. The key to combining is by making sure the fragrance families are in harmony or else you'll become a mal-odious scent.

Perfume lasts longer when sprayed on pulse points, which are the wrists, behind your ear, on the neck, inside the ankles, behind the knees, the crooks of the elbow, and at the bosom. Fragrance rises, so put your scent on from your feet to your shoulders.

Reapply fragrance approximately two to three times throughout a long day.

When wearing perfume, your scent should only travel about an arms length from our body.

### Bathing Scent Solutions

Bathing is not only a time to cleanse, but also an opportunity to renew and revive your body. This can be accomplished by adding fragrance to your bath or shower time. Spoil yourself a little by purchasing your favorite scent. Indulge in a warm bath with fragrant bubbles. When you emerge, spray on a light body mist, then cover yourself with fragrant lotions. I spray towels with the body mist, so I'm wrapped in a huge fluffy towel that smells wonderful.

## Sleep Chic

Add opulence to your resting time with lovely linen sprays. Many beautiful linen scents are available to either give your sheet a freshly washed aroma or a sexy alluring scent (for those intimate occasions with your husband). If you keep them stored by your bedside, you'll opt to use them more often. Try spraying your sheets with linen spray or your favorite perfume and then iron them. The heat will permeate your fabric with that lovely fragrance. You will have a heavenly sleep.

## Candle Power

Fragrant candles are calming, romantic, and posh. Place them in the bathroom while preparing for a spa experience. When entertaining, I love the atmosphere candles create. It seems as though shallow chitchat transforms into intimate conversation the minute the candles are lit. My husband and I enjoy them during our romantic evenings alone.

## Travel Candles

The travel candles that come in the aluminum containers with the tops for easy packing are a joy when I'm spending days away from home in a hotel. While burning, the candles fill the air with exotic scents and the calm of home.

## Home Fragrance

Every house should have a signature scent. It is inviting to enter a fragrant home. No matter what medium you use, the fragrances in your home tell a lot about your style. My home has a subtle floral aroma. Fresh flowers in bright, beautiful colors always fill my rooms. The bouquets please the eye and the olfactory senses simultaneously. Search for the little intimate places in your home where you can add fragrance. Your bathroom soap dispensers are a great place to begin. The choices for pleasantly fragrant antibacterial soaps are vast. I'm especially fond of raspberry or lavender scents. Many cleaning supplies now come in sweet smelling fragrances also. My bathroom tissue even smells great from using scented tissue cartridges. Fragrances can do so much to enrich your living space. Some scents have been said to possess the ability to prevent germ and sickness from spreading.

## Bug Beater

Moths and others clothes chewers are a terror to any wardrobe. To beat the bugs, hide little lavender sachets or wrapped bars of lavender soaps throughout your home. Lavender scented drawer liners work well too. You will save your dearest cashmeres and silks and come out smelling like a rose. Well, more like a geranium but you know what I meant.

## A Fragrant-Feel Better Trick

A really good feel better, pick me up and make me happy trick is to change the aroma of your surroundings. Remove old shampoos, body products, perfumes, even cleaning products, and laundry detergents and replace them with new scents. Since memories cling to even the faintest smells, renewing your aromatic environment will help you begin with a clean slate.

# Lifestyle Enhancing Scents

Use the following list as a reference as to which sprays, essential oils, or other carriers of fragrance can enhance the intervals of your life.

**If you are relaxing:** lavender is the best choice.

**If you are studying:** the scent of basil helps clear your head. Coriander helps you to concentrate and rosemary is helpful to your memory.

**For brainstorming:** Frankincense, bergamot, and rose (which is said to increase your alertness) are useful for inspiration.

### Bedroom scents

For sleeping: Lavender or Chamomile

For couples: It's said that Jasmine is a sweet aphrodisiac.

**If you are entertaining:** step lightly. Strong scents can be distracting. Some fragrances could ruin the taste of the food you're serving. For just the right smell to add an air of excitement, try a bit of cinnamon. Sprinkle a little clay sage to spark the atmosphere.

**Fragrances that Help Heal & Fight Germs**

**Tea Tree Oil:** Helps heal cuts & scrapes. Also helps prevent germs from spreading.

**Eucalyptus:** When my son Ryan was congested as a baby I put eucalyptus oil in the humidifier in his room. It helped him heal naturally.

**Peppermint:** It is a quick perk up. Peppermint tea helps soothe unsettled tummies.

There are many essential oils that can be added to a humidifier or diffuser. It's important to use the proper type of diffuser as some simply burn the oil and create a scent whereas others heat the oil and add subtle mental enhancements. For example lavender and lemon oil mixed together stimulate the brain and promote focus. Other oils help cure various ailments. Try visiting your local health store and research the oils that you use at home to enhance the atmosphere as well as improve your family's well being.

**Scented Seasons**

Use these aromas to keep your dwellings in tune with the season no matter what the weather is dong.

Springtime: Juniper, Lemon, or Lime

Summertime: Grapefruit, Mint, and Cucumber

Autumn: Spiced Apple, Amber, Vanilla, or Sandalwood

Winter: Ginger, Cinnamon, Orange, Pine, or Frankincense

The fragrances you filter into your environment effect your mood, thought process, health, social events, and your general well being. Put careful thought into how you can use fragrance to enjoy life. Perfume your surroundings with vibrant smells that denote your joy of living. Entertain, relax, and live with "good scents" and your life will be filled with an air of sweet success.

# CREATE A COLLAGE

Designing My Life to Enjoy:

## Fragrance

**Use the layout on the following page to design your vision in this area. Get glue sticks, magazines and cut out words and pictures to create an Enjoy Life Collage.**

Do you dream of having a vanity full of your favorite scents? If you engaged in a perfume purchasing frenzy, which scents would you buy? What do you want your home to smell like – fresh flowers, cinnamon, pine? Create a page that illustrates your desire to enjoy great scents.

*Designing a Life to Enjoy*

# CREATE A COLLAGE
LifeCoach2Women.com

# CHAPTER 13

# Enjoy

*art*

*"Art is not for the cultivated taste. It is to cultivate taste."*
*– Nikki Giovanni*

Art is my passion. My family is full of art lovers. My friends love art and I am positive that you are an art lover as well. That may sound foreign if you have fallen victim to the rigid scholastic idea of what "art" is and what "art" is not. Scholars should be commended for making the simple subject of art complex. Many help foster the belief that only the scholarly and moneyed can recognize and appreciate art. I strongly disagree. Every culture, ethnic group, and people within these groups regularly enjoy and create art. When a man wants to convince a woman to spend the rest of her life with him, he offers her culinary delicacies in a special atmosphere infused with music and excitement. Years ago, a young college man sent words of love, adoration, and commitment up to the balcony where his true love stood. What is a wedding but the combination of music, food, pageantry, tradition, and dancing? Holidays find family dining rooms over laden with food, the air charged from the exchanging of family photos, memories, and stories. See how art is evident everyday? But if you pay attention to academics, you would never see art this way.

After hearing, "I just don't like art" from enough people, I developed a broader definition of art. I consider art to be anything that sparks your senses (sight, touch, taste, hearing, smell) and invokes a thoughtful or emotional response. When we employ that definition rather than academic dogma, art is as varied as the individual observing it. Art then becomes any form of painting, sculpture, literature, music, cuisine, photography, or dance. Can you see how easily and regularly you partake in art?

As I asserted, you are definitely an art lover. Now is the time to become an art connoisseur. Connoisseur comes from the Latin word "cognoscere" – to know. The words cognition or cognitive are derivatives and each suggests an educated knowledge.

A connoisseur is someone who enjoys, discriminates, and appreciates the subtleties of art. We are just taking your love to a new level of enjoyment. Since we have established that you do in fact love art, the goal becomes the pursuit of expertise, appreciation, and discriminating recognition for the art that surrounds us everyday.

### Live with Art

Bring art into your intimate world by filling your home with art. Twyla Tharp offered the following perspective: "Art is the only way to runaway without leaving home." Only art whisks you away to a sunset beach while snowfalls outside your window. Only through art can you enjoy the poetic lyricism of Pablo Neruda or visit the azure Brazilian coast via the hum of a bossa nova band. With our new definition, many things can be art. The only requisite is that it produces a reaction in you. I am always moved by children's drawings. I find their liberal use of color and questionable shapes utterly charming. Adhering to academic rules, few museum curators would feature childish scribbles in a museum exhibit, but I believe they should be matted, framed, and displayed with the same pomp and circumstance, given to a Monet. Since you are not a museum curator, what's stopping you? Fill your home with photos, print work, and that odd sculpture produced at camp. Is it less artistic because you thought it was a bowl until your little art protégé told you it was a vase? Add color to your walls and to your life with living creations from today.

### Energize the Atmosphere with Music

Music is an invisible force that heightens and brightens the atmosphere. Give music a tangible presence in your home. Vary your selection. I love smooth jazz and dance music. Music has associative qualities and hearing a certain song is often a reminder of a certain moment or event. Invite the world into your home through melody. Try classical chamber music or Latin samba, lively jazz, and note the subtle change within your four walls. Music makes the mundane magical. Imagine washing dishes or doing chores with the aid of some Latin rhythms. You might begin dancing or singing and envision yourself somewhere else, perhaps transformed to another country or on the beach. Sometimes it's nice to allow the music to take you away.

### Develop a Home Theater

Public television is a wonderful resource for artistic exploration. Cable and commercial programming is geared for the masses, whereas public television focuses on "the discriminating viewer". Their corporate mission is to educate, enlighten, and entertain viewers on a more intellectual level. I have seen Broadway plays that never toured in my area. I've seen movie adaptations of classical literary works and spectacular performances by world famous artists whose peak has passed. Find out what's on your local PBS station. You will be pleasantly enriched and surprised.

### Venture Out with Art

Bringing art home is great, but the adventure of exploring art requires an inquiring mind and the courage to willingly pursue. Your home may be full of books, with walls covered with prints and paintings, but art is a living, constantly reproducing force in this big world. The excitement of a live performance, seeing the actual brush-strokes on a canvas or being in a place discovered in the pages of a book is indescribable.

The energy of a live performance is a hundred times more kinetic than a movie or TV screen. The audience is always charged in anticipation. People are milling in the foyer discussing what they have heard about the production from others. The theater is the last frontier of culture and gentility as the coat check girls and the ushers wish you a pleasant evening. As you settle in your seat- you wonder-will everyone remember their lines, will it start on time, how will the staging look? Despite the number of previous performances, it always feels like the first time. You become a part of the production and the audience's anticipation fuels the cast. It is electrifying. When the production is over, I never want to leave. You hear people whistling the tunes and discussing the scenes as they head to their cars. Nothing can match it. I have forgotten many movies along the way, but I can remember every ballet, play, musical, and symphony I have ever seen.

Live performances also have the added advantage of spontaneity. Movies are glossed over, edited, and cut for celluloid perfection. The frill of the live performance is, anything can happen. Friends and I attended an outdoor performance of Shakespeare's "A Midsummer's Night Dream". First, it rained on us. Then, they moved the production to a very small tent. The close quarters, combined with their soaked costumes, produced an aura of silliness from the actors –it was a comedy after all. One actor was holding a lantern, and hit another actor in the head-hard enough for everyone to hear.

The actors and the audience burst into laughter while the offended person did a brilliant job of continuing his lines, although what he immediately said was not in the original manuscript. We were a part of something that will never be duplicated nor soon forgotten.

Seeing a major work of art has the same exhilaration. I can't remember the number of times I have seen the Mona Lisa by Leonardo da Vinci in books, on posters, and postcards, but I will always remember seeing it at the Louvre in Paris. Before entering the chamber where she was hung, the tour director warned us of the ensuing spectacle, but the reality of it was altogether surreal.

In the middle of the room, a crowd of people were pushing and shoving, while security guards attempted to maintain order. Flash bulbs were as blinding as on Oscar night. I thought someone famous was in the room, but it was the painting. The throng of people was at least seven rows thick. How would I ever get to it? At first I was cautious (and scared) until I realized what I might miss without drastic measures. Aggressively, I tucked my purse under my coat and pushed.

Eventually, I made it to the front. I was right in front of her—the famous painting of an ordinary Italian woman with the extraordinarily enigmatic smile. It was beautiful. I could see the true colors, the brush-strokes and the thin layers of oil paint that produced luminous skin tones described in art books. I could almost touch it. The seven-hour flight across the Atlantic was worth that one moment, and I would do it again.

Venture out into the world of art, because there are so many avenues to try. Start local, but dream without boundaries. Be willing to go across the globe to see those who manifest their experiences through creativity.

### Study Art

Art is a discipline. It takes perseverance to make exploring and learning a lifetime pursuit. As with anything else, you just need to determine your interests and focus. Becoming an expert in any one area actually broadens the base of your learning experience. If you love Cubist art, you can attend a class and study Picasso and Braque. Maybe you would read Picasso's biography and see the movie on video. Maybe you would be further inspired to visit Picasso's homeland in Spain and relive the things in his homeland that inspired him.

On this trip, you might become aware of the cultural richness of Spain's music, food, or language and branch out into those areas and pursue greater knowledge of that. You could investigate Picasso's contemporaries and their works, such as Gertrude Stein, Ernest Hemingway, and F. Scott Fitzgerald. You could fine-tune your travel, gearing toward cities with museums that feature his work. You begin your journey on one road, but it leads you to many others.

**Try Art for Yourself**

There is an artist inside of you screaming for escape. In school, your grass had to be painted green, not orange the way you liked it and you were reprimanded for coloring outside the lines. Once we left kindergarten, we put our crayons away and were taught to neglect our aesthetic tendencies. The subject may have been revisited when confronted with the mandatory art class. There you were told to like Monet and ignore country watercolors. Once you left high school, art was put aside again as an erudite pursuit. It is not surprising that art is dead to you. No one ever brought life to the subject by allowing you to follow your desires instead of forcing rules on you.

Now that you are an adult, you can learn, explore, and color any way you like. Take a watercolor class and paint the sky pink if you want. Nowadays there are many pop-up paint classes that are at local restaurants. They offer hundreds of paintings to choose from, you can select a design that matches your style or a particular room in your home. It is so easy to sign-up online and let your creative juices flow. Take a ballroom dancing class and swing until you're dizzy. Learn to develop film in a lab. Join a creative writing workshop. Find a poetry reading and read; enter an art competition, audition for a local play. Try a little art on for size, you might find that it's a perfect fit.

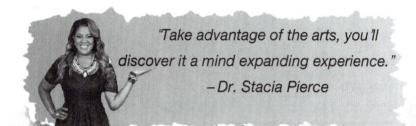

*"Take advantage of the arts, you'll discover it a mind expanding experience."*
*— Dr. Stacia Pierce*

### Travel with Art

Every city has an artistic style and heartbeat. Depending on your personal interest, make it a habit to see art in every travel destination. Some locations are known for architecture (Chicago), textiles and crafts (Phoenix), plays and musicals (New York), orchestras (Boston), food (Paris), or dance (San Francisco). Art makes travel a pleasure, because you can taste something new and exotic. I have a travel ritual. I always visit a museum or art gallery and a shopping mall. My husband on the other hand loves food, so no matter where we visit we have to try a new place.

My goal use to be to find something that served as a reminder of that city for me based on its particular personality. In Washington D.C., I went to a performance of Shakespeare because of the notoriety of the theater. The cerebral, conservative aspect of the play seemed a perfect match to D.C.'s straitlaced atmosphere. San Francisco, on the other hand, is edgy and ethnically diverse. Now that I have visited certain cities several times, now I frequent the places in those areas that I know and love. My family now feels more like locals in certain cities as some employees know who we are as soon as we arrive.

### Find Art Partners

Art has a magical quality, the more minds that digest it, the longer it lives. Sharing your love of art with others is the beginning of lifetime friendships. We often pick one best friend, and load him/her with every detail of our lives. Like a diamond, you should have facets of your life and friends for each facet. An art partner's main purpose is to share, explore, and discover art with. I have many in my life. A co-worker has season tickets to the local theater.

Our conversation consists of whether she's going to the next production and if she liked the last one. Comparing notes and critiques is the extent of our relationship, and that's fine. I always see a certain university student at the local bookstore poetry reading. Our relationship begins with a smile upon recognition. Sometimes we look at each other and laugh when we find a poem unusually amusing. I have friends with whom I discuss the latest movies and the upcoming plays and we attempt to see them together. We usually continue the theme in our gift-giving. I went to the ballet for my birthday and she saw the musical Evita for hers. We begin or end the night with a sumptuous meal. Sometimes our conversations extend to the deeper things of life, often they do not. We just enjoy the art of life.

My daughter, Ariana, is also my art partner. When we can coordinate our schedules, I try to find an interesting activity. One year, we saw a production of the Diary of Anne Frank. I had never read the book in school, so I was as excited as she was and it was a learning experience for the both of us. We found the book, she was reading it along with her schoolwork and she told me how it compares to the play. I'm glad that we had that time together, and I also realize the play was a visible reinforcement of what she read.

### Become an Art Collector

I love beautiful art. If I see a piece that I love, I buy it. Sometimes I purchase originals, other times prints and also limited edition pieces. My home is like a gallery. I have art on pretty much every wall. Don't feel limited to one style. I love modern and more traditional art as well. Some pieces are framed, some have baroque frames while others are modern. I like certain colors and when I see them put together in a way that speaks to me, I buy it. Sometimes I commission local or emerging artists to paint me an original. I can tell which are extremely talented and may become famous or popular in the future. I like to get one of their pieces before the price goes up and hold on to it as the value increases.

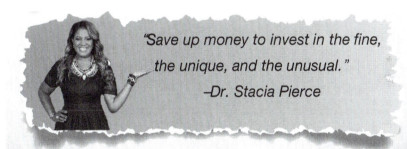

"Save up money to invest in the fine, the unique, and the unusual."
–Dr. Stacia Pierce

### Relive Art

Being taught well by my art mentor, I have three indispensable tools at my disposal. The first is my travel journal. I keep a cultural file. This file contains articles about museums, paintings, composers, theaters, etc. I never know when I might be in a city and want to know what to do when I go. I keep articles about auctions, retrospectives, and artist biographies that I might get around to reading. I even found an article about how to attend an auction. You never know when it will be useful.

I also keep a cultural journal. I keep the program of the play, musical, and exhibit I attended. I then write my own personal critique. You never know, I may see a small production in a local theater that becomes the next Broadway sensation and I'll be able to see what I thought about it. Besides that, I can look back and review all of the things I experienced. I keep this along with my travel journal.

# CREATE A COLLAGE

Designing My Life to Enjoy:

## Art

**Use the layout on the following page to design your vision in this area. Get glue sticks, magazines and cut out words and pictures to create an Enjoy Life Collage.**

Do you need to add more culture in your life? What type of performing arts would you prefer to see? Would you like to have inspiring art pieces in your home? Create a page that illustrates your life of class and culture.

Designing a Life to Enjoy
# CREATE A COLLAGE
LifeCoach2Women.com

# Personal

## *Muse*

# CHAPTER 14
# Enjoy
## Saturday Mornings

*"Use your weekends to create memories, prepare for an opportunity, take an adventure or explore the world around you."*
**–Dr. Stacia Pierce**

What do Saturday mornings mean to you? Shall I sit and spin you enchanting tales of the Saturdays of old where ladies lunched with children in tow, to fulfill their social fancies? There once was an era in which Saturdays were dedicated to refinement and manners, and tradition were second nature. The world we live in today has seemingly abandoned the fine Saturday rituals that fill our lives with an enjoyable quality. Well, not to worry, I've outlined infallible remedies that will save those Saturdays drained of refinement and illustrate how to reach a life well-lived.

Though it takes true commitment to enjoy each day, I have especially made a commitment to enjoy my Saturday mornings. I refuse to allow my Saturdays to be ordinary. I refuse to stay in my comfort zone. Come out of your comfort zone on Saturday mornings. Get a local map of your city. Highlight your normal Saturday route. Then in big letters label that area "My Comfort Zone." Now, create a goal to travel outside your comfort zone and make your life extraordinary. Saturdays are a good day to explore and find the treasures that make life precious. I make good use of those precious moments.

With the many responsibilities that demand my attention, I truly cherish the Saturday mornings that I have free. I try to fill those days with exploration, while nurturing the relationships with my family and friends. Use your Saturdays to spend time with your spouse, children, or other loved ones. Dub it as an "exposure day" to expose yourself and your loved ones to a cultured agenda and activities that breed refinement. Here are some simple insights to saturate your Saturday with warmth and enlightenment:

**Window Shopping Revamped**

Here's a new twist on your usual trip to the mall. Take a day to learn how ladies on the next level shop. Go see, touch, and smell luxury clothing and accessories. Try on something that is above your present status. Expose yourself to the finer side of fashion. Be willing to journey to high-end retailers in order to examine the designer sections during your visit.

**Art Museums**

Just taking twenty minutes to stroll through one of these safe havens for masterpieces will send your creativity soaring. Before your departure, stop in the gift shop. Museum stores are usually well stocked with exceptional books and collectibles.

**Bookstore Browsing**

There are some days when our family lacks the stamina bedded to tackle the crowds in the mall (can you believe I just said that?) Anyway, on those days we spend the morning in a quiet bookstore. Free from time restraints, we sit down, read books, talk, and get a bit silly at times. On occasion, an author is appearing, which makes our bookstore adventure extra special. Bookstores are a wonderful place to sit and browse. Although, my browsing usually has a turning point and I end up purchasing a few books to add to my library. Try a Saturday morning with the kids or a friend, your mate or alone at the bookstore. Look for books on subjects you've been meaning to investigate but haven't had the time.

## Big Breakfast

If your life is anything like mine, you probably don't have time for a big elaborate breakfast each morning. Health wise, we have learned it is better not to overload ourselves first thing in the morning. Setting my heath consciousness aside there are just days I long for a good old fashioned southern breakfast like the ones my Mom used to cook on Saturday mornings when I was growing up. So on those mornings, before the family arises, I'll hit the kitchen in full motion. First, the table is set and decorated. Then, I pull out my beautiful, colorful serving dishes. The menu consists of my family's favorites. Fresh fruit trays, gourmet French toast with a touch of cinnamon, turkey sausage, eggs scrambled with onions, cheese, and bacon bits, grits with cheddar cheese, and a dash of pepper. Naturally, fresh squeezed orange juice is the beverage of choice. As the aroma saunters up the staircase, it awakens all of the sleeping Pierces and leads them to join me in the kitchen. Take a Saturday morning to rise early, pull out your best dishes and make a fancy breakfast. Think of some stimulating conversation starters. If you don't have a family to cook for invite a friend over, they'll enjoy the hospitality.

## Kid's Pick

For those who want to walk on the wild side, allow your children to create your Saturday agenda. Before you have a Kid's Pick day, set your mind and attitude for what's ahead. When my children were young, I'd allow them to pick whatever they wanted to do (within reason) on that Saturday morning. My daughter usually wanted to shop, dine out, and catch a movie. My son's choice was usually a day filled with fun and play. His ideal Saturday included a trip to a children's play place to enjoy every game, eat pizza, and buy a new toy. Allowing the kids to make the agenda for the day expresses that you deem their interests important, and makes them feel quite special. If you don't have children, give someone you know with children a free Saturday morning. Pick up their kids early in the morning and keep them until late afternoon. It's great practice and a great gesture.

## Nearby Destinations

Is there a place in a nearby city that has treats and treasures that you adore? When I lived in a smaller city, approximately one hour away from my hometown there was an incredible place for me to hunt for deals. One of my shopping partners and I would rise very early, pack up the kids, and head on our way. We were ordinarily some of the first people to arrive, so we get a jumpstart on the crowd. Sometimes even traveling a short distance can be refreshing. Every city has a mind-set, so to expand your mind or stir your creativity a short drive just might be the ticket. See if you can find yourself a nearby destination that offers you an outstanding shopping or a sight seeing opportunity. Venture off to a fair, art show, or ethnic festival. Find various events to attend on Saturdays. Your experience will equip you with "behavioral know-how," therefore giving you the confidence to perform well in a variety of settings.

### Vision Casting Day

Every person in my home owns a Millionaire's Dream Book, including our children Ryan and Ariana. Mine are adults now, but when they were younger they planned their future as well. Don't underestimate the comprehension of your children; you'd be shocked at what they can do with the proper tools and instruction.

We all have busy schedules, so when we can, we gather our magazines on a Friday night, and then rise early on Saturday. We start by reading through all of our magazines, and then we go back through them and tear out the sheets for our Millionaire's Dream books and vision boards. Looking like artists at work, we sit around the kitchen table with glue sticks, scissors, and a wastebasket near by. Music normally fills the air and we engage in meaningful conversation regarding our perfect Planner finds. By the time noon rolls around we stop for lunch and a treat, which is often homemade cookies. Do you have a purposeful ritual in which your entire family can participate?

### How to Create your *Vision Board*

Planning your future is a great way to spend your time today. Using your *Millionaire's Dream Book* will help you improve your experience, it will help guide you to specific areas of your business or family life. Vision boarding is great for short term goals, it allows you to post up images on a larger scale and view them daily. The Millionaire's Dream Book on the other  hand is divided into sections, it is filled with Photo Collage Pages for you to paste images and words that express a specific dream or desire you have in specific areas. Each page has a subject heading followed by a spot for you to write your Collage Title. The Collage Title is your opportunity to personalize the page and build your collage around your goal project. Your choice of pictures and words will magnetically be directed after placing your title at the top of the pages.

Pictures bring your dreams and ideas to life. Look in magazines, brochures, and advertisements for pictures or use actual photos you may have already. To make completing your dream simple, I provided quotes on each page that you can say for each area of your life. As you meditate on your faith photos and affirm these words over your life, you dreams and goals will be drawn into existence. For further clarification, listen to the "Frame Your Future" CD that I included in the packet when you buy your Dream Book.

### 3 Ways to Host a Vision Party
1. Group Party
Break out the magazines, turn up the music and invite a group of your friends over.

2. Personal Party
Grab a friend or partner and have a one-on-one party to share your visions and dreams with.

3. Brainstorming Party
If you are a manager or leader over a team of people at work, use the Millionaire's Dream Book as a brainstorming tool to generate new ideas for special projects.

# Other Ideas for Saturday Mornings:

- Take a long walk.
- Ride your bike.
- Read a good book.
- Have breakfast in bed.
- Meet a friend for breakfast.
- Write in your journal.
- Spend the morning visualizing your dreams.
- Write letters to friends you've been out of touch with.
- Thumb through a stack of magazines.
- Watch old classic movies.
- Schedule a Saturday to entertain your dearest friends with a party that will change their life.
- Catch up on your scrap booking. Pull out all those old pictures; get creative in placing them in scrapbooks.
- Listen to motivational audio all morning and take action notes.
- Play in your makeup. Come up with some new techniques.
- Sit with the kids and read books together.
- Play games or work a jigsaw puzzle.

Use your Saturdays to love, laugh, and learn. Taking the time to explore and learn will ensure that you create a fulfilling life. Carefully orchestrating your Saturday mornings will create life experiences for you and your loved ones that are legendary.

# CREATE a COLLAGE

Designing My Life to Enjoy:

## Saturday Mornings

**Use the layout on the following page to design your vision in this area. Get glue sticks, magazines and cut out words and pictures to create an Enjoy Life Collage.**

What interesting parts of your city have you yet to explore? How can you use your Saturday mornings to prepare for an opportunity that doesn't exist yet? Think of ways you can use Saturdays to create lasting memories with your family and friends. Create your journal page displaying the joys of your Saturday mornings.

Designing a Life To Enjoy
# CREATE A COLLAGE
LifeCoach2Women.com

# CHAPTER 15
# Enjoy
## Girlfriends Adventures

*"To get the full pleasure of joy, you must have somebody to divide it with."*
*–Mark Twain*

Girlfriends: these are the people with whom you share the things you love; like shopping, antiquing, tea parties, or a good book. These are the ladies you call when you've found great stationery or the perfect shoe. As women we long for meaningful relationships and special people with whom we can be ourselves. We long for girlfriends that we can have good times with laughing and discovering, healing, nurturing. These rare jewels are hard to come by. Every woman needs to be a part of a group of authentic girlfriends who don't compete and compare, envy or care about status. Their main concern is to be friends. Girlfriend adventures are all about bonding. They cause the people involved to open up, laugh, and talk freely. I do know that you must use great wisdom when choosing who will surround you, but I also know that your friends can make everything about life a little more fun. I want my life to be a celebration, so I've chosen to make it a priority to develop meaningful relationships. I believe many people simply don't enjoy life because they keep all of their relationships in the shallow realm. Girlfriend adventures will help you rescue shallow relationships and take girlish delight in the unexpected. Venture out and participate in exciting adventures with those who celebrate you.

### Celebrated or Tolerated: A Journal Exercise

Make a list of all of your friends, then meticulously review it and determine the purpose and depth of each of these relationships. Next to each person's name place a "C" or a "T." "C" means this person celebrates me and vice versa. "T" means this person tolerates me and vice versa. Veer away from tolerated relationships and pour your energy into the relationships in which you are celebrated. Armed with your new list of comrades, consider new ways that you all can get together. I love to entertain, especially for just the girls. Glean from some of the following ideas to create outings for your adventuresome group.

*"When you invite fun people whom you adore, there is always the possibility of something exciting happening."*
*—Robyn Hambro, Former director of American Vogue offices in London*

## Planning a Girlfriend Adventure

Gather the Right Crowd

Carefully examine your invitation list to make sure you have chosen a group that mixes well together. Don't be afraid to branch out. Every now and then, add new people that you would like to get to know.

### Tell them Ahead of the Game

You will have greater participation if the people invited know way in advance of your upcoming get together. Don't become rigid though; there are times for you to take a spontaneous approach to entertaining your friends.

## Money Matters

Make whatever event you plan cost effective for everyone. If you are aware of the financial status of your friends, take it into consideration as you plan.

## Calendar Considerations

Most of my friends are extremely busy. We stay connected through cell phones, e-mails, and letters as we bounce from plane to plane. There have been a few spontaneous get-togethers, but for the most part I plan my calendar and schedule my getaways in December before the first of each year. Be mindful of everyone's schedule. It may take a bit of creative planning, but you'll get better results when attending your girls gathering is convenient for everyone.

## Girls with Goals

When mapping out the festivities for the girl's great escape, choose a theme that speaks to all of your goals. Do all of you want to become more cultured? Then get away to a play. If everyone needs to relax, rent a cabin or find a less-than-busy beach house. Should the entire group be in search of adventure, go on a safari. Or for a less dangerous adventure, you could hire a guide to lead you on a nature hike. Got a bunch of sporty ladies? Gather the troops for a ski trip or a weekend of extreme sports. Whatever suits the fancy of you and your girlfriends, go for it. During your time away, discuss how you all can realize the goals you have in mind. Then go out and have the time of your life. Good, clean fun with good, true friends will enhance the quality of your life immeasurably.

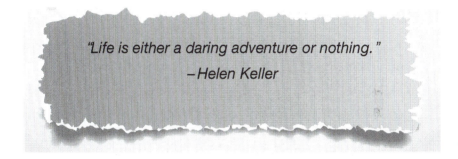

*"Life is either a daring adventure or nothing."*
*–Helen Keller*

### Girlfriend Themes
Makeup for Lost Time

Several years ago, I planned a "Girlfriends Night In." It served as a time of relaxation, socializing, and beauty updates. The night consisted of frolicking in cosmetics, learning the latest makeup techniques, and discovering what colors were hot. Give each guest a beauty book and a makeup goody bag. Pull out all of your beauty magazines so everyone can pull the pictures that reflect their image goals. The magazine finds will then be used for the collages in your *Success Journals*. Come up with a dress code that is casual and chic. Take lots of pictures and make the night memorable.

### Bookstore Bonanza

There are times when I pair up with a girlfriend I haven't seen in a while and go hunting at the bookstore for wonderful cover-bound treasures (any excuse to get to the bookstore will do). As we enter we start in the same section, but as the time lingers, we find ourselves scouring through the shelves for books that feed our individual passions. Before you know it, hours have passed, and then we hit another bookstore and start the process again. By the time we are done (many heavy bags of books later), we are ready for food and conversation. So off we go to some swank café, or chic bakery, a nearby restaurant, or whatever eatery our taste buds lead us to. Upon reaching a destination, we rest our laurels, eat our "crumpets," drink our tea, and relentlessly share about the day's events. Together, we enthusiastically discuss all of the treasures we found and review which things on our dream lists we are working on next!

### Divine Dining

Sometimes girlfriends get together merely to gab. My friends and I usually add a little flair to such impromptu gatherings, by meeting at a really private, upscale restaurant. Selected establishments call for more formal dress, but in many of them you can be business casual. The privacy and elegance of hybrid dining causes you to be able to talk more freely, while enjoying the ambiance. Search for restaurants in your area that have an upscale flair. Before you take a friend, dine there yourself. Check out the menu, will your friends enjoy the selections? Your girls' night out will become a disaster if everyone hates the food.

Frequent restaurants that will make special accommodations for you as well. Usually this type of service is dependent on your relationship with the establishment. For one of my recent dessert gatherings at a local restaurant, I requested specific desserts for each of my guests ahead of time. Each dessert was to be delivered to them with a special note card from me. The vibrant colors used in the table setting were a reflection of my personal style. For the tea selection, I chose my preferred herbal flavors. Even when you are hosting outside of your home, put a little pizzazz in the event by adding your personal touch.

### The Power of Tea
Many times when we hear of women having tea, it seems like a delicate cliché. But more often than not, there is a sense of strength at these gatherings. Invite

friends over for tea and revive age-old traditions that cause ladies to bond. Over tea, you can swap life stories, and receive valuable advice. In addition to the tea, pour into each other the support and love that develops courage, and empowers women to do great things.

### Start Your Own Girls Group

Set a meeting time and gather the ladies together based on a common interest. If you have a love for a certain hobby, like crafts, sewing, or even deep sea diving, begin a group that shares your love. Throughout the world, women meet together periodically to celebrate their friendships and their lives. The togetherness that is created in such groups of girlfriends is unbelievable. You may choose to meet once a month or once a year if great distances separate you. More important than the frequency in which you meet, it's the abundance of full-filled rituals that enrich your time together.

### DNT (Do Nothing Together) Day

*Julie Sutton said it best: "friends are those special people you can enjoy just doing nothing with."* Take time to be with your friends without a rigid agenda. Just sit around each other's house, or ride with one another to do errands. Just being in the company of good friends can be inspiring. On do nothing days you'll be amazed at the intensity of the conversations. Without the need for noise, you can more easily enjoy the presence of good friends. Now I'll be honest, very seldom do I have "do nothing" days with my friends. Those days just don't come around very often. This is partially due to my choleric (must be achieving something worthwhile at every moment) personality, and partly because of the business of my life. However rare, such times have designed memories that are forever cherished. The time shared during those days solidified and built lifelong friendships.

If you are excited about the girlfriend adventures, but fear you haven't a friend to share them with, I have help for you too. The following fail-proof principles will help you find and keep quality friends.

# Finders Keepers

## Locating & Maintaining Good Friends

### 1. Look for Them

There are great people out there, so don't give up on the idea of having a true friend. You must show yourself friendly if you are going to build positive relationships. Reach out to ladies at your church or on your job. Participate in inspiring women's events hosted in your area. Try to build friendships with those who are amusing and intellectually stimulating.

### 2. Show your True Colors

Be honest about who you are and what pleases you. Don't put on a facade to please others. If you are never yourself, you will never know if your friends like the real you.

### 3. Be Fair

Don't take advantage of friends, especially if you have the stronger personality. Be considerate of their time and needs also.

### 4. Don't Gossip!

You'll never build trust necessary for a good friendship if everything your friends say to you goes right out the door. Resist the temptation to tell the secret of another.

Likewise beware, if one of your friends always has the latest gossip, you can rest assured, they are "sharing" about you too.

## 5.  Learn to Lean Without Being a Burden

Learn how to get support from a friend without being needy. Don't use your friendship as an outlet to consistently whine about problems. Yes, in times of trouble, or when you need encouragement you should be able to call on your friends. On the other hand, if all of your conversations are negative, it's time to change your ways.

## 6.  Don't Steal from, Stab or Step on Friends

If you borrow money pay it back. Don't backstab your friends. Use integrity and restraint when dealing with their husbands, their network, and their job ideas.

## 7.  Find Ladies with Similar Interests

If you don't like heights and your new friend is an expert mountain climber, your social agendas will probably clash. When friend searching, make sure you have a few things in common with those you want to associate with.

## 8.  Invest in the Building

Do your best to make time for your friends. Invest in them. Periodically, if I come across an item that I know one of my friends would love, I purchase it and send it to them. Nurture your new friendships so they can grow.

## 9.  Find Out What's Important to Them

Don't forget their birthday. Know the birthdays of their children. Be thoughtful of their interests. Congratulate them when they achieve a goal. Take advantage of every opportunity to celebrate them.

## 10. Love Thy Neighbor as Thyself

It's the golden rule and it hasn't failed yet. Don't do to a friend what you wouldn't want done to you.

## Enjoy Your Girlfriends

Revisit the basics of childhood joys and gather the girls for an outing. Include adventures in your lifestyle, and you will build a network of good friends to help you navigate through the twists and turns of everyday living. Times with your girlfriends are irreplaceable and piece-by-piece they make up the moments in which you enjoy life.

# CREATE A COLLAGE

Designing My Life to Enjoy:

## Girlfriend Gatherings

**Use the layout on the following page to design your vision in this area. Get glue sticks, magazines and cut out words and pictures to create an Enjoy Life Collage.**

What adventures can you come up with for you and your girls? How would all of you look? What would you wear? Decide what type of bond you want to create on your adventure. Do you want to laugh together, learn together, or share your hearts? Create a page that shows the happy times ahead with you and your girlfriends on a great adventure.

Designing a Life to Enjoy

# CREATE A COLLAGE

LifeCoach2Women.com

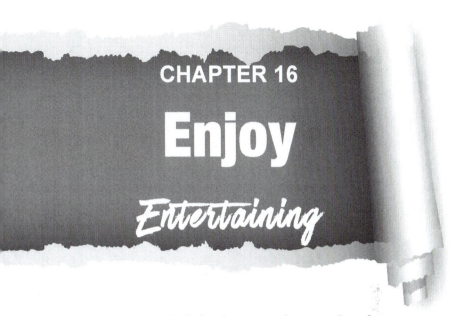

# CHAPTER 16

# Enjoy

*Entertaining*

*"Take pleasure in bringing people together for a good time."*
**-Dr. Stacia Pierce**

To me, entertaining is another way to exercise my passion for beauty and to celebrate others. It's a time of socializing and it allows me an outlet for my creative expressions. When asked to define entertaining, I close my eyes and conjure up images of warm hospitality and good food. I see family and friends gathered around laughing. I imagine candles, colorful linens and a lifetime of memories with the people I love. I agree with Diana Vreeland who said, "It's totally wonderful when you can experience an evening at someone's house."

I love festivities and fun times with people who are dear to me. I have found it essential to experience the smooth rhythms of engaging in conversation and easy delicious meals. My home has become a celebration center of honored guest and elaborate fun. Planning, not cost, should be your main concern when hosting a celebration. Inventiveness will more than cover for any lack of resources. View the events in your life with fresh eyes. Orchestrating ordinary happenings in an extraordinary way turns a regular day into a grand occasion and weaves meaning into the fabric of our lives.

I have a passion for parties. My inner interior designer creeps out often. Consequently, I find myself turning every special day into a fascinating event. I host about 8-9 parties a year at my home for various occasions. I encourage you to take some time to entertain throughout the year. Entertaining others is a great gesture of love. It can also be a form of networking. Even if you are a novice at entertaining, use the upcoming information as a springboard for your own ideas. Entertaining brings lasting rewards. Armed with this repertoire of entertaining expertise, you can begin to pin the act of hospitality down to a fine science.

> *"All good hostesses artfully manage to make their parties look effortless."*
> *-Nan Kempner*

# How to Entertain Successfully

### Plan

Everything should be thought out from comforting your company to serving scrumptious food. Put your personal touch on every aspect of your entertaining from the menu to the parting gifts that you distribute to your guests as they say good night. Invest the time to thoroughly plan your event and you and your guest will have a wonderful experience.

### Create a Theme

A celebration without a theme is a sunken effort. You must begin with a theme. It will direct your path for all of your party planning decisions. Every portion of the event should flourish from your theme. The flowers, the place setting, the invitation to even the type and color of the food served should all come together to make a lasting impression.

### Write a Guest List

Even for my children's birthday parties, I delicately compile a guest list. The best parties have the most interesting mix of people. The people you invite will contribute to the type of atmosphere that is set. Vary your selection. At times you may host an intimate gathering with only your dearest friends. On other occasions host an event where most of the guests have not met. This is a fun way to spark new friendships.

### Choose your Decorations

Decorate according to your theme. What colors will be used? Will there be flowers or other types of centerpieces etc.? Write down everything you need to purchase.

### The Menu and the Dining Experience

First ask yourself questions. Will your gathering be formal or informal? Will you serve an entire meal or just hors d'oeuvres? Next, determine how you can mirror your theme with the place settings. Make sure you have enough of your flatware utensils to serve food and to eat with. List the types of food that complement your theme and décor and create your menu. Based on the number of guests attending you can gauge the amount food you need. Make adjustments for any special dietary needs of your guests. Create a menu that you believe everyone will enjoy, but don't be afraid to try new and interesting foods. Everything that is served should complement each other. The finger foods should flow with whatever is being served at dinner. Strive to make your dishes as decorative as they are delicious. Think not just of how the dish will taste, but how it will be presented.

*"I have discovered that people, for the most part, like wonderful, simple food."*
*-Mrs. Betsy Bloomingdale, Philanthropist*

### Invitations

The anticipation that precedes your event is mostly created by the invitations you send. The style of your invitations gives your guest a hint of what joy is to come. Especially with formal gatherings, put great thought into your invitations; they set the whole tone for the event. Remember to put all vital information on the invite: Who, what, when, where and how. Invitations should also indicate if there is a dress code and contact information to RSVP.

## Plan the Clean Up Before the Party Begins

Either hire someone to help you clean up or solicit a few friends to stick around and tidy up after the event is over. Don't allow the dread of clean up to dampen your spirits before the party begins.

## Choose your Attire

Dressing for the occasion is part of the fun. As hostess, your outfit should mimic the air of the entire event. You must stand out from the guest to be recognized easily, especially for larger events where all the guests may not know you personally. I heard one host who entertains a lot say that she always wears something bright, so she can be easily spotted by her guests.

## Leave Yourself Plenty of Time to Get Ready

Have a little quiet time before your event. Take an hour to sit down and sip some tea, look over your décor and recheck your guest list. Finally, put on your makeup, do your hair, get dressed and calmly wait for your guests. The success of any event relies on the hostess. If you aren't in a frenzy when your guests arrive you can't be fired up with enthusiasm. On a similar note, keep the evening as relaxed as possible. Your attitude as the host is contagious. Don't flutter around in hysteria when little things arise. Keep a calm head, even if your cheese cubes are starting to melt.

*"A host is like a general; calamities often reveal their genius."*
*-Horace, a Roman Poet*

## House Guests

When inviting friends in for an overnight stay, let lavish attention and beautiful surroundings spoil them. Outfit your guest room with fresh flowers, a small basket of snacks, motivational readings, miniature toiletries and soothing fragrances. For breakfast serve a marvelous tea and fresh bread. Their comfort should be your top priority. Attempt to make your house guest feel as cared for as members of the family.

## How to Create a Special Atmosphere

One of the secrets to making any occasion special is creating an atmosphere that says, "You are welcome here." It's usually small touches that make a big difference. Start with fresh flowers, flickering candles, a beautifully set table, soft background music, fragrant potpourri and a great bubbly host. The following are a few hints to help you create the right atmosphere for your next gathering.

## Music

Music helps to eliminate feelings of awkwardness. It eases your guests upon their arrival. Be sure the type of music you choose to play complements your theme. I keep several kinds of genres on hand for my gatherings. Choose a style that encourages the feeling that you desire, select upbeat music if you want to get the crowd excited or happy. If you want a more relaxed atmosphere, select a calming playlist. Keep the volume soft enough so neither you nor your guests are straining to talk over the music.

## Play a Game

Choose a few great games that are appropriate to the type of event that you are hosting. Relationships are also dependent upon play. Review the guest list and their personalities, then find a game that would be fun for everyone. Gathering your friends together just to play is a gift that continues long after the party is over. In a state of play, you unclutter your mind which makes you more creative. Hosting playtime will provide an outlet for your guests that will help them perform better in other areas of their lives.

### Greetings

Provide a warm welcome for your guests, so you take the jitters away at the door. Besides, a warm welcome shows your guests how excited you are to have them attend.

### Lighting

The type of lighting you choose will determine how people will relate to each other. If you are having a large group and you want them to mix and mingle to get to know each other, keep the lights bright. The brighter the lighting the more talkative people will be. If you're going for a serene more intimate atmosphere, dim the lights and candlelight will do.

### Seating

Move your furniture around to provide an atmosphere that promotes conversation. Groupings of furniture that faces each other are excellent for getting people to talk. Never set any chairs off to the side or by themselves, because some person will probably grab it and end up isolated the whole night. Remember that it is difficult for people sitting in a row next to each other to converse. Not only is it uncomfortable but often the person is just too close. Set two sofas facing each other or place your sofa in front of some chairs to encourage conversation.

For example, you could say "Tiffany, meet Sabrina, she's an interior decorator with a clever eye for antiques; (then turn to Sabrina and say) and Tiffany here collects antique plates."

*EXAMPLE 1:*
"Everyone, meet Sue who just wrote a great new book."

*EXAMPLE 2:*
'Meet Ann, she's a chef at the new restaurant everyone is talking about."

Now, the two who just met have something to discuss. As a host beware of being trapped in a long discussion. You must keep moving, it's your duty to greet and share with as many of your guests as you can.

## Keep the Conversation Going

See yourself as the verbal liaison amongst your guests; especially if they don't know each other well. Have stock of lighthearted conversation starters and ideas in the back of your mind. Before your event, think of some thought-provoking questions that line up with your theme. Whenever the time is right, ask the questions to your guests and encourage them to chat. Dead air is a surefire way to kill a party. As the host, it is what you bring to the table that creates enjoyable moments at your gathering.

*Entertaining Ideas and List*

**Glamour Getaway**
**Tea & Intimacy**
**Christmas Tree Gathering**

## Happy Birthday to You

As you plan birthday celebrations for those close to you think of the activities that they enjoy the most and the things that are most important to them. Then try to create a theme that would suit their taste or benefit their life at the time.

Entertaining is another form of good-hearted hospitality. It allows you to share your heart and celebrate those you love. Use your home to entertain. Throw grand dinner parties, casual lunches or intimate teas. All of those provide a happy refuge for loved ones to build a bond that is endearing. Develop a talent to make each guest feel special. It demonstrates that you are committed to a lasting relationship with those closest to you and to begin a meaningful relationship with those who are not.

On the surface, it may seem that hosting an event is a service that you do for others. Looking more closely at these delightful experiences and fine times we make a surprising discovery. As host, whatever amount of ourselves we pour into entertaining, we receive just as much benefit in return. Entertain from the heart and give a gift of celebration that continues forever.

# CREATE a COLLAGE

Designing My Life to Enjoy:

## Entertaining

**Use the layout on the following page to design your vision in this area. Get glue sticks, magazines and cut out words and pictures to create an Enjoy Life Collage.**

Would you have more events if the décor in your home was exactly like you wanted it? How about throwing your self a huge birthday party? Maybe you are more inclined to entertain through intimate gatherings with a few close friends. What about dining alfresco at your place? Create a page that entertains you and outlines your social future.

# CHAPTER 17

# Enjoy

*Dining Out*

*"Life itself, is the proper binge."*
**-Julia Child**

We live in an era of restaurant chic, where atmosphere, distinction and elegance are all a part of fine dining. Quality food, outstanding service and fine china arranged like a museum display collaborate in order to entertain you. In years past, I have had many opportunities to dine in the finest restaurants as well as those nostalgic holes in the wall that serve fabulous food. Both types of eateries leave me in awe of how the restaurant experience can broaden your life's perspective. Each extreme incorporates food, service and ambience.

You add flavor to your life-style when you take a moment to enjoy being enchanted by the servers, chef's delicious meals and rich décor which fine dining provides. Never again think of dining out merely as a way to eliminate your hunger and shovel down nutrients. Instead, think of it as a culinary fling, a chance for you to socialize, please your palette and savor the ambience. If that sounds like a tall order, join me at life's dinner table and make note of the following points you can snack on.

## Great Ways to Enjoy Dining Out

### Enjoy Your Favorite Spots

Cafes, bistros and a good restaurant usually describe my favorite spots in the world. The creative décor, as well as varieties of food along with sheer ambience lures me to such places again and again. Quaint little eateries are easy to socialize in. I adore great deli's, petite cafes and snazzy bistros nestled in culturally rich neighborhoods or busy downtown areas. They add another dimension to my tradition of dining out.

### Enjoy the Food

Many restaurants today offer stellar food choices. During this age of celebrity chefs and artistic food arrangements, do not neglect to absorb your entire dining experience. Don't be in a hurry to just eat, but choose to enjoy the luxury of mouth-watering foods and their presentation. You can learn so much from the impeccable attention that is given to detail in a fine restaurant. So open your eyes and enjoy!

### Enjoy the Décor

Once you reach your delicious destination, look around you. These days restaurants are turning to top designers to create customized dining emporiums that stimulate all of the senses, not just the palette. When appropriate, carry a camera and take snap shots of stylishly designed interiors. I believe a feast for the eyes is worth capturing. I always do a bathroom check because it inspires ideas and informs me of the character of the owner.

### Enjoy the Service

Great service in luxurious environments offer a time of rejuvenation and peace. If you long for such an experience, get off the beaten path of fast food and journey to an upscale eatery. You'll be more than pleased when a tasty feast and grand hospitality are at your service.

### Enjoy your Company

Don't overlook the importance of mealtime conversations. Some of my best dialog and brainstorming sessions have occurred while dining out. I strive to have rich experiences with my family and friends. I agree with Alexandra Stoddard who said; "The richer our private lives the greater our self esteem." Avoid committing the common travesty of sitting across from your dinner partner(s) in silence. It's amazing to me to see people dining, without saying a word to one another. What a waste. Be careful not to chatter so much that you are unable to chew, but an insightful verbal exchange will always add life to your dining. A famous traveler once said, "One should enjoy the company they eat with or choose to dine alone." I most certainly agree.

### How to Converse

Try not to be too loud or boisterous in a dining establishment. You should be able to participate in a fulfilling discussion without making too much of a joyful noise.

### Enjoy People Watching

I love the practice of dining and people watching, especially when I am in New York City. Everyone interacts with such panache (well, maybe not the cab drivers). Boasting scores of eateries that are right in the midst of the NYC social set, it's easy to find restaurants that are dedicated to seeing and being seen. No matter what city you are in, a "happening" restaurant is one of the best places to people watch. The best of the "people-watching" restaurants have somewhat of a celebrity vibe and continue to draw new and regular patrons due to the "who's who" crowd that dines there. Eating in these types of establishments is usually loads of fun because you get to observe and meet intriguing people.

Before I was a part of this posh crowd, I would look for style clues. I checked to see what type of handbags the ladies were carrying and how they've cut their hair. I noticed how they introduced themselves to one another, what seems to be the nature of their conversation and what they order. By watching how celebrities carry themselves or how the elite interact in your town, you too can learn dining elegance. Now as my own status has increased I am thankful for those moments of social learning.

### Keeping a Dining Journal

I am an idea collector, so when dining in a restaurant that has been creatively thought out, I make a note of little tricks and treasures to use when entertaining at home. Keep track of what you eat and where you have utterly indulged. Record the experience, what stood out, notes about the décor, the name of your waiter who was exceptionally good, etc. Write down how you ordered your steak and what you had for dessert. Always carry pen and paper while dining out; you never know when an incredible idea may strike.

## Dining Etiquette

I have penned a few lists of the most important dining tips that are worth more than money can buy. Review them carefully and use these pages as a reference lest you ever forget. Mastery of these social graces will equip you to make every dining experience a culinary triumph.

## Dining in a Private Home

To be a dinner guest at someone's home is both a privilege and an honor. In order to dine with confidence and grace, it is important that you learn the finer points of etiquette that come with dining in a private home. Dining as someone's house guest is much more intimate than dining in a restaurant and therefore calls for a little different etiquette.

# How to be a Great Dinner Guest

 Always RSVP as soon as possible

 Make sure that you (and whomever is accompanying you) know the names of the host and hostess.

 Get directions prior to the event if necessary.

 Take your invitation with you to the event.

 Be punctual, never early. If you are running late, call and inform your host of your estimated arrival time.

 It is generally good etiquette to bring the host a gift. A nice bottle of sparkling juice or flowers are fine. If you do bring flowers, make sure they are already in a vase, so the host doesn't have to take time to find one.

 Let the host lead the way into the dining room and direct you to your seat. Place cards may be on the table to direct you as well.

 After being seated, observe the host before touching anything on the table. When your host picks up their napkin, you may place your own on your lap.

If this is a large dinner party, cordially converse with the guest on your right and your left. If the host does not introduce the guests to one another, introduce yourself to those on each side of you.

 Never discuss gossip, dieting, calories, personal problems, allergies, ailments or controversial issues while dining.

 Say "Thank You" when you are served.

 Eat what is set before you. If you try something you don't like, it is okay to leave it on your plate. Never complain about the food.

 Neither wolf down your food, nor pick at it. Eat at a moderate pace.

 Don't go for second helpings unless offered. To decline a second serving that is offered, simply reply "No thank You."

 First compliment the host on the food before asking any questions about it.

 When dinner is finished, don't "eat and run". Plan to stay at least thirty minutes after dinner unless you informed the host (prior to the event) that you would be leaving early.

Take your cue from the host as to when your stay is over. Say a pleasant farewell before you leave.

 Write a thank you card to the hostess. In your writings, make mention of the host and share your appreciation for the opportunity to dine with (him, her or them). Be sure to mail the card within a few days following the event.

### Formal Dining Etiquette

Most of us have seen the classic scene in the movie "Pretty Woman" where actress Julia Roberts attempts to eat escargot and sends it flying across the room. Baffled by which silverware to use, she is rescued by her host who discreetly points out the correct utensils to work with. Relieved, Julia's socially challenged character flashes her host a naïve and gracious smile. Although it was merely a movie, this scene is all too true. In today's modern world, most women are not taught how to dine in upscale establishments. Many ladies not used to full service restaurants, look clueless when it comes to dinner etiquette. You don't have to be caught off guard. Use the pointer's here to add polish and finesse to your upscale dining.

# Signs of an Upscale Restaurant

- **Tablecloths over the tables**
- **The menu does not include prices**
- **A maitre d' seats you**
- **The meal consists of three or more courses**

# The Dining Lesson

## 1. Seating

- In an upscale establishment, a maitre d' will usually lead you to your table.

- Once you reach your table, don't sit down until your host sits down.

- Use free time to introduce yourself to those around you and so on. This will make you more relaxed and confident.

- Once your host is seated, you may sit also by entering to the right of your chair.

- If a gentleman helps you with your chair, be sure to say thank you.

## 2. Tableware

The amount of tableware before you will depend on how many courses you will be served. Regardless of the number of courses, some simple rules apply.

**Silverware**- Silverware always follows the same rule. Start from the outside and work your way in towards the plate. Knives and soup spoons are placed on the right and forks on the left. The seafood fork is the only fork ever placed on the right. If there isn't one there at the start of the meal it will be presented on the plate with the seafood. If you use the wrong utensil, simply ask the waiter for another one before the next course. When in doubt of which to use, watch your host.

 **Plates**- When you are the first to be seated, you will see two plates. Your service plate (also called a charger) will be directly in front of you. This plate is larger and merely for decoration. Your courses will come on their own plates and be placed on top of the charger. Just before the entrée is brought out, your charger will be removed. The second plate you will see when seated is your bread and butter plate. This plate is smaller and sits on the left side above your forks. Any rolls or finger foods you are served can be placed on this plate. Your bread and butter knife is smaller than a dinner knife and rests on the bread and butter plate.

 **Glasses & Cups**- Glasses and cups are always on the right above the knife. The iced tea glass will be to the right of your water glass. The rest of the glasses are to be used starting with the one furthest to the right and working your way in. Each glass is removed when the course assigned to it is finished.

 **The Napkins**- your napkin can appear in one of three places: on your charger plate, above your forks or below them.

**FORMAL table setting**

## 3. Dining Preliminaries

- A formal dinner consists of five or more of the following courses: soup, fish, sorbet, a main entrée of meat or poultry, salad, dessert and coffee.

- Dinner begins when the host places their napkin in their lap. In some full-service restaurants, the maitre d' may go around and arrange a napkin in each diner's lap.

- The maitre d' will share the house specials and then take orders beginning first with the host. When the meals are served, they are served from the left. Dishes are removed from the right. Drinks are both poured and cleared from the right.

- After all the first courses have been served, the host should give the guests a few seconds to pray over their meals.

- Any condiment or other dishes that need to be passed should be passed to the right.

## The Courses

**Soup**- The soup may either be presented in a soup bowl or in a shallow soup plate with wide rims. Using your soup spoon, sip the soup without making noise. When you get towards the bottom, you may tip the bowl to get the last little bit with your spoon. When you are done with this course, place your soup spoon on the soup plate beneath your soup bowl.

**Salad**- To eat your salad, use your salad knife and fork. If a salad knife is not available, you will have to use your dinner knife. When you have completed your salad, place both your salad knife and fork across your salad plate in the "finished position" (think of the 10 and 4 positions on a clock). If you had to use your dinner knife, do not place it across your salad plate or it will be removed. Instead, place it across you bread and butter plate to use it later when your entrée is served.

**Fish**- Fish is either served baked or grilled, as whole or in portions. The fish knife can be recognized by the notch in its blade. This notch is used to separate the bottom and top halves of a fish when it is served whole. The fish fork can be easily recognized because it will be the same distance from the plate as the fish knife. When eating fish, it is proper to remove small bones by using your fingers.

**Sorbet**- Sorbet is not to be confused with the dessert course. It is merely a frozen fruit juice, (not containing milk solids) which is used to remove other flavors from your mouth and cleanse your taste buds. It is served in a small dish with an underlying plate. Though most people don't eat it, Garnish (a green leafy looking thing), may be served on the plate and can also be eaten to cleanse your palate.

**Main Entrée**- just before your entrée is served, the waitperson will remove the charger plate. Your main entrée will generally consist of a piece of meat or poultry and a side dish. The side items will probably be a serving of rice, potatoes, a specific vegetable or a vegetable medley of some sort. Eat slowly and carefully. Be sure to cut your meat one or two bites at a time.

**Dessert**- When dessert is served, use your dessert fork or spoon that is lying directly above your plate. Use only your spoon if you are served pudding or ice cream. For cake, pie or other pastries, use your fork. When you have finished, once again put your utensils in the "finished position" to be removed.

**Coffee**- Coffee may or may not follow dessert. During this time it is okay to request tea if that is your preference.

**Toasting**- During a formal dinner, toasting may also follow dessert. In this case, the person initiating the toast should stand. Guests may raise and sip from either a glass of sparkling juice or their water goblet for the toast.

**Concluding Dinner**- When dinner is over, the host will indicate that it is time to leave the table by removing their napkin from their lap and placing it to the left of their plate. Never put your napkin on your plate or leave it in your chair. The guests should follow the host's lead. Dinner is now over.

### Restaurant Etiquette for the Host

As the host you must understand that your guest will be looking to you for guidance and direction. It will be your responsibility to initiate most actions and to control the course of the event. The following guidelines should help you truly become the "hostess with the mostest" whenever you dine out.

- Always keep in mind the needs and comfort of your guests.

- Know the name of all your guests and their spouses.

- If you are making reservations, put them in your name.

- Arrive early at the restaurant, introduce yourself to the maitre d' and choose the table you want to sit at. Look over the surroundings and familiarize yourself with the menu.

- You may want to make arrangements for the bill before your guests arrive. The management should be able to take your credit card information then. Then they can discreetly present you with the check and sign at the meal's end.

- Be seated in the most prominent place. Indicate to others where they are to be seated if they look lost.

- Introduce your guests if they are unfamiliar with one another.

- Pick up your napkin and place it on your lap. This signals to others that dinner has begun and they can pick up their napkins as well.

- Take the initiative to order first. Remember others may be taking their cues from what you order. If this is a new place for your guests, suggest a few entrees.

- Cordially converse with all those present. Help keep the conversation flowing smoothly, but do not hog it.

- Model good table manners.

- When dessert or coffee is served, request the check. Handle the check without comment if you are paying for your guests.

- Leave a generous tip of 20% of the pre tax bill.
- After the meal, escort your guest to the door and thank them for joining you.

# CREATE a COLLAGE

Designing My Life to Enjoy:

## Dining Out

**Use the layout on the following page to design your vision in this area. Get glue sticks, magazines and cut out words and pictures to create an Enjoy Life Collage.**

Do you have a list of restaurants that you would like to dine at across the country? What dining experience have you always dreamed of? Are you ready to take the challenge of trying new foods and flavors? Create a page that illustrates where and how you would enjoy dining.

*Designing a Life to Enjoy*

# CREATE A COLLAGE
LifeCoach2Women.com

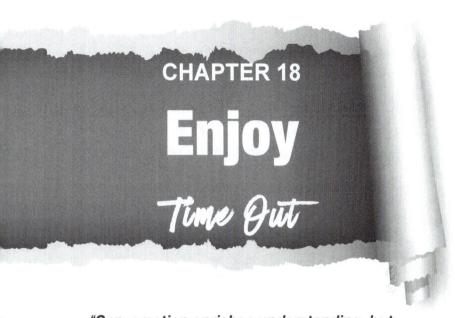

# CHAPTER 18

# Enjoy

## *Time Out*

*"Conversation enriches understanding, but solitude is the school of genius."*
*-Edward Gibbon*

Every week I encounter busy women who feel like they are juggling fine china. They run from school projects, to tending to their marriage and home, to taking care of aging parents, children and friends, to working full time in and out of the house. Due to this continual race, they are becoming fatigued, disappointed with themselves and sometimes even desperate. After talking with and sharing the hearts of the overwhelmed, I felt obligated to use these pages to share the precious insight I gained long ago. "You are not much use to anyone else if you don't feel good yourself."

Solitude is one of life's most valuable treasures; it gives us a "feel better" freedom from the demands of others and times to delight ourselves alone.

One year I was running so much that I didn't take time out to care for my health. I slacked on my vitamins and didn't eat properly. Burning pure adrenaline, I was headed for trouble. Finally, one morning, I awakened to find myself too sick to even get out of bed. My health was hanging in the balance and I had plenty of time to think. It took many days of resting, listening to audios on health and healing, as well as a lot of prayer for me to get back on my feet.

**From this attitude altering experience I learned:**
- Never neglect your body's warning signals.
- Take a break from your rigorous schedule to do something you absolutely enjoy.

As you feel yourself approaching the point of no return, it's time for you to get away. I love to travel. Nevertheless, the "get away" I'm referring to in this instance does not require a suitcase or passport. It plainly requires that you get alone. Solitary leisure time affords us the opportunity to reconcile our thoughts, deal with our emotions and consider our direction in life. Time out gives us a peaceful moment to revisit how we really are and what we want out of life.

During your little "get away" you can be totally honest with your feelings without pretenses. Though it may seem that you don't have a moment available for solitude, you must make time for quiet moments away.

### Find the Time to Get Away

We all could use an extra 24 hours in our week, but the fact remains that everyone must work with the same amount of time. When finding time to get away, you must make the most out of the time you do have. If need be, change your habits to give you time you need. Get up a little earlier or go to bed a little later so you can have some time alone.  No matter what your responsibilities, you can make time for you. Sometimes I rise at 5:00am just so I can write in my journal and pray while the house is quiet. Create time for yourself. Where there's a will there's a way.

### Take Time Out to Live

Live while you're still alive. Even when you are not alone, slow down enough to really experience your life. Enjoy your husband, your children and your friendships.

Don't let your life fly by. Your life is a party, so participate in the celebration. Don't wait until it's too late. Absorb life and make every moment count. Be aware of time snatchers such as TV and nonproductive, lengthy phone conversations. Don't allow those habits to flush your future down the drain.

Take on a solitary pursuit to accomplish something you've always wanted to do. Participating in an activity alone increases your self-confidence. Start a hobby or take a class. Engage in something that is centered on your interests. Journalize about how you can use your time better, to give yourself a few moments of solitude. Then, write a list of things that you will do with your newfound time for yourself. Then get out your planner and schedule those activities on the calendar for the next ten months.

## Ideas for your Great Escapes

- **Discover a place you've never been before- a museum, library, café or bookstore.**

- **Take an overnight retreat. Find a nice hotel and give yourself the luxury of time to study, pray, meditate, sleep in and watch a few good movies.**

- Schedule a professional pedicure.

- Go for the gusto and get a full body massage.

- Get a makeover at a department store.

- Curl up with an inspirational book.

- Take a long quiet walk.

- Indulge in a relaxing, candlelight bubble bath.

- Take a pleasure course like flower arranging, painting, basket making or a foreign language.

### Make a Collage

I love creating collages and thank God that I wasn't distracted or persuaded to back off of such a child-like activity. Instead, I stayed sensitive and open to discover why this expression was so important to me. Now, my *Millionaire's Dream Book* helps others to frame their future with words and pictures, using the collage technique. Now that tool is being used by thousands across the country to make a profound impact on the outcome of their lives.

### Hiring Help

To live out your dreams and enjoy your life with your sanity in check, you may need to hire some help. Most women believe that somewhere in the distant years to come they will finally be wealthy enough to hire help. In some instances, you may need to hire help in order to have the quiet time you need to come up with a million dollar idea. You don't have to be rich to get some assistance, but you do have to be creative. A possible shift in finances could make life more enjoyable. You may choose to eat out less often so you can afford to have someone watch the children for a few hours a week while you take a break. Many cleaning services also have very reasonable prices. Maybe you could save $30 per week so you could have someone come in once a month to do some heavy cleaning. Or it may be within your means to hire a cleaning service or someone to cook a few times a week and you just never thought to follow through on it.

# LESS IS MORE

Take a look, it may not cost as much as you thought to hire help.

**Chef Check**- For example, if you eat out three times per week with a family of four you probably spend $180, which is enough to hire a personal chef to go to the grocery store and prepare three meals.

**Order Out to Organize**- If you are very disorganized and lose things frequently, you probably have a cluttered home. Approximately $250 (which you probably have spent replacing things you've lost) can get you a 2-4 hour session with a professional organizer who can give you solutions.

**Dressed to Thrill**- Have you ever wasted $20-$30 worth of gas driving back and forth across the city in search of the perfect outfit? That same amount of money can get you the expertise of a personal shopper. Better yet, some high-end stores offer shopping assistance free of charge.

Hiring someone to assist you with menial tasks like cleaning, to very important tasks like cooking meals for your family or caring for your children, will help you accomplish more. As my kids were growing up, I had a childcare assistant who cooked daily, as well as a cleaning service to help me maintain my home. My schedule becomes very hectic at times and their assistance helped me to balance all of my responsibilities and spend my time doing things I cherished like playing a game with my son, writing letters with my daughter or going on a date with my husband. Don't be ashamed to hire help. The proper assistance will help you and your family enjoy life more.

### Take Time Out to Look at Yourself

Just as you must take time out for your mental health, you must take time out to look after your outer appearance. Your skin, hair, teeth and clothing all play a part in your overall feeling of well being. Invest the time to look fabulous. Not only will your self-worth skyrocket, but those around you will value you more. Someone who takes care of themselves always makes more pleasant company than someone who just lets themselves go.

Look over yourself from head to toe. Peer into your own eyes; examine your mouth, teeth, hair and nails. Observe your skin, review your outfit. Are there any areas that are not up to par? Did you notice any areas where you have really let yourself go? Are there just a few minor improvements you would like to make? After you complete your observation, begin with the first area and ask yourself a couple of questions:

**1. Why does this area look like this?**
**2. What can I do about it?**
   **After answering these questions begin to make a plan. Pay close attention to your hair, nails and teeth.**

**Hair:** If you don't know how or have time to properly care for your tresses, hire a professional. Though daily care at home is a must, schedule weekly or monthly appointments to maintain good "hair-esteem." Get professional advice on a style that fits your face shape, personal style and is easy for you to care for.

**Nails:** Gel or acrylic nail tips are a great way to keep your hands looking well kept. If artificial nails aren't your thing, make sure your nails are clean and well manicured.

Chapter 19 includes inside tips on great home manicures.

**Teeth:** Your teeth affect your appearance. A healthy smile is a woman's best asset and a great smile by brushing at least twice a day for at least two minutes. Then, follow up with floss. Finish up by gargling with mouthwash, which kills both bacteria and bad breath.

Take time out to find beauty secrets just for you. If there are things that you hate about your appearance, learn how you can make the most of it. Get educated on new make-up techniques. Discover the habits of beautiful people. It is not always blatant disregard for the proper image that causes us to appear less than desirable. Often times it is a lack of beauty knowledge that holds us back from getting gorgeous. Many of the maintenance practices and beauty secrets of today's most attractive women have been passed down for generations. If you do not have a heritage of beauty do-gooders in your family, the heritage of self-care must begin with you.

## Beware of the "Scruffies"

A scruffy look happens on those days where your personal image has gone amuck. It's those "bad overall image" days, when you feel like you should apologize for everything from your hairstyle to your outfit. Scruffy times are those moments when you realize you look completely unkempt, but you say, "I'm just going to run in the store for a minute. I hope I don't see anyone." Of course you know whenever you do that, you always run into someone, right? Anyway, we all are guilty of having an occasional "scruffy day" on our record. Be concerned though if you notice that your scruffy days are becoming commonplace. Have you become accustomed to looking undone? If so, there is something wrong. You may need to enhance your image upbringing and know-how so that you have the necessary information to make a polished presentation.

On the other hand, your constant scruffiness may indicate that you need to get in touch with your emotions. Your lack of upkeep may be your subconscious warning you that there is something wrong with your state of mind. It is unnatural for you to have little concern about your personal appearance. If you just don't care what you look like you may be suffering from low-self esteem, loneliness or depression. Get to the root of the problem, then work your way to a well styled, well balanced you.

### Lights, Camera, Take Action

Decide what you want to look like. What type of image do you want to portray? Get ideas for image improvements from stylish friends who always look well put together. Many high fashion magazines and movies have everyday ideas to incorporate runway favorites. Watch what the stars are wearing. Attending a fashion show or enrolling in a beauty school is also another way to update your knowledge and make an image overhaul.

Taking time out for you to look your best makes life interesting and fun. Do what it takes to look good and feel great about your self. The well put together woman experiences life as an adventure with many windows of opportunity and exciting days ahead. No matter what your schedule, you must carve out time each day to care for yourself.

## Take Time to Play

Creative people put high value on fun because it enables them to soar in their other pursuits. Playing keeps you sharp, but it also keeps you flexible; says Lenore Terr MD at University of California at San Francisco medical School. Create a budget to put away money in a "fun fund". This way, you have the financial freedom to spontaneously participate in fun activities. Participating in playful activities gives you an outlet to relax and regain your creative juices.

Recall the activities that you loved when you were a kid, then find the grown-up equivalents to play today. After completing an intense project or successfully weathering stormy times in your life, give yourself a break. Happy times of play restore your ability to hope, believe, love and laugh. The events of your life give you some of the best sources of inspiration and information. Add splashes of color to your life with fun events like; weekend shopping trips, outdoor sports or visiting a new restaurant in a nearby city. A world full of all work and no fun, is colorless and dull.

## Start and End your Day with Quiet Time

Take time out at both ends of your day to get alone and meditate. Prayer, reflection and godly meditation each day will help you stay well grounded and weather any storm that life may bring. Thoughtfully consider your day. What good things happened? If it wasn't that great, what can you do to make tomorrow better? It is always within your power to improve your situation. Even if it's only by your attitude, there is something you can do to increase the quality of your day.

I know that solitude doesn't last forever. Eventually, we all have to emerge from our oasis of quiet time, into the real world of deadlines, demands and the general work of life. I've learned though, that if you take time out routinely and make the most of your leisure time, you will be one hundred times more effective when it's time to put your hands to the plow.

# CREATE A COLLAGE

Designing My Life to Enjoy:

## Time Out

**Use the layout on the following page to design your vision in this area. Get glue sticks, magazines and cut out words and pictures to create an Enjoy Life Collage.**

How and when would you love to get away? Evaluate your image. What do you need more time to improve? What solitary activity can you pursue? Design your days of great escapes. Create a page that shows exactly how you will use your time out.

Designing a Life to Enjoy

# CREATE A COLLAGE
LifeCoach2Women.com

# CHAPTER 19
# Enjoy
## Pampering Yourself

*"The care of oneself shows the ultimate respect for God's creation."*
*-Dr. Stacia Pierce*

While preparing to write this book, I used my "time out" to journalize a lot. I reviewed all of my accomplishments and how much I honestly enjoy my life. I moved to examine the lives of successful women in many different arenas. When trying to find a common jewel among the treasured women of our day, the insightful information I found brought me to the following conclusion: "Most people cannot do great things, because they don't live great private lives." A great private life begins with the proper care and keep of you.

Fall in love again with the ritual of being a woman and enjoy the pampering practices that were created with you in mind. I always say that great lives are woven with care. A part of that fabric for fabulous living is mastering the art of personal pampering. To create a life worth enjoying, you have to learn to be unavailable sometimes to tend to yourself.

Don't belittle your pampering time; it is a necessary practice for success. Make appointments with yourself. A portion of your private life must be devoted to doing things that refresh your mind and relieve tension. When we are constantly deprived of private, personal care, we become resentful and eager to get away from everything and everyone. Working in a few minutes here and there to pamper yourself will cause you to feel refreshed and in control of your life.

Become your own best friend and engage in activities that make you feel beautiful and loved. The level of your self-esteem and confidence is reflected in how you take care of yourself. As you begin to add pampering time into your lifestyle, decide what your personal beauty philosophy will be. Personally, I've decided that I am important enough to give myself the royal treatment. If I appreciate the measure of beauty that I have been given and treat myself like I'm gorgeous, I'll get gorgeous results.

You possess your own special beauty. Personal pampering shows your love and appreciation for the wonderful creation you are. So, get gorgeous! Here are a few tricks of the trade that beautiful women of all ages practice to look great all the time. They work for me, so I will share them with you.

## Real Beauty Secrets of the Gorgeous Woman

1. **Laugh a lot.** The sour-face look is never lovely.

2. **Wash and moisturize your face morning and night.** Clean, soft skin is in no matter what season it is.

3. **Use makeup to highlight your unique features.** Just because it's different doesn't make it a flaw.

4. **Be kind to others and yourself.** Self-hatred destroys your ability to see your unique beauty.

5. **Look fresh and rested.** Give your body the proper rest. There's nothing pretty about exhaustion.

6. **Self-discovery is key.** Knowing who you are and what you want out of life gives you an air of confidence that looks marvelous.

7. **Enjoy life everyday.** Unhappiness weighs on the soul and wilts the beauty of the woman who bears the weight.

8. **Get the golden arches.** Stylish eyebrows are worth their weight in gold. Have a professional arch your eyebrows. Nicely done eyebrows add polish and character to the structure of your face.

9. **Facials are fabulous.** Once a month get yourself a facial or get it professionally done. This deep cleansing pampering tactic will increase your face value.

10. **Do not compare.** Don't always be afraid that someone is prettier than you. Beauty is individual. Just put your best face forward and you'll be surprised at how gorgeous you look.

To enjoy pampering means that you take out time to appreciate yourself and indulge in the little things that bring you pleasure. Pamper yourself mentally by staying in a positive environment. Subjecting your self to unnecessary, spirit-dampening experiences show poor judgment and low self-regard. Discover what things really make you happy. Doing what you love is an awesome way to pamper yourself from the inside out. What do you love to do? Make a list of the things that you absolutely love doing. Next to it, make a list of things you should be doing to take better care of yourself so that you can continue doing the things that you love.

**To point you in the right direction, I'll share my list:**

> ➢ I love to walk on a beautiful day and look at landscaping.

> ➢ I love to read early in the morning especially in the springtime and summer with the breeze coming in the window.

> ➢ I love my bed being made right after I get out; the room instantly comes to attention.

> ➢ I love the look of perfume bottles glistening on my vanity table.

> ➢ I love being intimate with my husband.

> ➢ I love the word excited.

> ➢ I love creative people and spending time conversing with them.

> ➢ I love to shop.

> ➢ I love entertaining and planning events.

> ➢ I love make-up.

> ➢ I love bookstores and books.

> I love facials, manicures, massages and my absolute favorites—foot massages and pedicures.

> I love getting Thank You letters.

> I love journaling.


Now, decide to add more of these life-lifting activities to your typical day. Cause them to be intertwined into your life until they become a natural part of your weekly routine. Stop and close your eyes and think about something you love.

**Taking Better Care of Myself**
- Floss my teeth twice a day instead of once

- Drink more water

- Eat 5-7 servings of vegetables and fruit each day

- Get a pedicure more often (I'm always on my feet speaking)

- Get more facials and body massages.

Follow a daily ritual that keeps you in tune with your internal cues. My daily ritual consists of taking out time for quiet reflection. This is my meditation time. Often I experience what I call the "Aha Factor", some idea or notion is triggered in my mind or an answer to a problem is revealed. This morning ritual brings me such pleasure. Not only does it get my day started right, but it often helps my agenda each day. My senses are fully awakened and I am inclined to see opportunities as they arise throughout the day.

Along with having a daily beauty ritual and keeping a proper beauty philosophy, there are some pampering practices that are a must as you make your way to an enjoyable lifestyle. Once a month, I spend time at a day spa getting a full body massage, pedicure, and an aromatherapy facial. Whenever I'm in the spa, I cut off my cell phone and rid myself of the priorities of others to take time to focus on taking care of me.

Before I had the luxury of going to the spa so often, I practiced the same discipline, just in the privacy of my home. Don't allow the amount of money you have deprive you of the luxury of pampering yourself. My monthly treat in those days would be to purchase a beauty book or magazine so I could learn how to do self manicures, pedicures and facials. My husband James and I would take turns giving each other full body massages....well, we still do, but now it's just for the fun of it.

If you have never been to a professional spa, put it on your dream list. Take action by calling around to get prices then begin to set aside money to treat your self. This totally indulgent experience will change your life. You'll see just how relaxed you can become when being pampered.

French women have a secret to always looking beautiful and well preserved. A part of their cultural practices include professional treatments. Many ladies begin around the age of twelve. Professional treatments are an important part of personal pampering practices.

### Body Massages

Treating yourself to a full body massage is the most wonderful experience. A good, professional massage will cause your body to totally wind down, relax and rejuvenate. Most people are a little intimidated at their first few sessions because they don't know what to expect.

# Making the Most of Your Massage

## 1. Ask questions
When you call to book your time, inquire about attire, tipping or anything else on your mind. Also, specify whether you want a male or female therapist.

## 2. Leave undergarments on if you prefer
When undressing for your massage, it is not mandatory that you remove your undergarments. However, even if you are totally undressed you'll always be covered, except for the area that's being worked on.

## 3. There's no rule you have to be quiet
If you prefer to talk that's OK. Keeping quiet seems to make the whole experience more personable and rewarding. I never talk, because it gives me time to think. Sometimes I even fall asleep.

## 4. Speak up immediately
If the touch is too rough or too light for you to enjoy, inform your masseuse of how you are feeling. Remember, this is your pampering time.

For most American women, a professional massage, facial or full body scrub is a rare treat; but that doesn't mean you have to deny your self of spa style treatment.

Even if you can't escape for the weekend or your spa budget is on the back burner, you can still enjoy head to toe treatment in the comfort for your home.

The designers of the greatest spas breakdown their establishment into different categories to ensure that the process of pampering of a client is well rounded and complete. I have done the same breakdown for you, to clue you in on top spa techniques. All you need to do is schedule a quiet evening, gather your ingredients and indulge yourself. If you take this approach, your home spa retreat will never lack luxury.

## The Home Spa Experience

### Sound

Fill the air with beautiful music. Sometimes when I do go to the spa, I take my own music and ask them to play it during my massage. Music without words is best. Find an instrumental collection you enjoy. Certain selections of classical music are very soothing.

### Sight

Pick a place in your home that is easy on the eye to do your treatments. Utilize a space that is uncluttered, clean and serene. If no place exists, clear the way so you can enjoy your spa day.

## Touch

During your pampering time, it is important that you wear clothes that are gentle on the skin and have an easy fit. Wear a fluffy cotton robe or beautiful cotton pajamas. Big fluffy towels are a joy to wrap up in. Anything you touch should bring additional comfort to your experience.

## Taste

Taste something delightful. Enjoy tea, a light snack or fruit juice. Once while at a spa, I was served fruit water, which was spring water with sliced oranges, lime and other fresh fruit inside. Sipping on a tasty beverage in a decorative cup adds to the delight. For snacks, cut up fresh vegetables and fruit and artfully arrange them on a tray.

## Smell

A pleasant aroma alone is therapy. Fill the room with fresh flowers and add scented candles all around. Treat your self to an atmosphere filled with fine fragrance.

# Your Spa Activities

### Take a Power Shower

In your quest to pamper don't over look what I call "power showers." Traditionally, remaining in the tub buried under a wall of bubbles for hours used to be my standard view of luxurious bathing. Today as my schedule becomes more and more hurried, I've incorporated this new style of showering to pour a little luxury in the wash.

An extended shower after working out, before bed or prior to attending a major event, can be a quick way to energize and rejuvenate yourself. For those who are presently committed to the tub experience, try a long, hot shower with fragrant gels and rich soaps.

Let the taps of the fresh water drops massage and relax your body. It's absolutely heavenly. You'll love it.

To draw the most from your power shower add it in as a part of one of your daily rituals. Before I host or attend a major event, I take an extravagant shower to prepare myself to look and feel my best. In the mornings, I meditate in the shower on my upcoming day. Many great ideas and products have come to me during my power shower time.

**Self Serve**

Pampering yourself by mastering this lady like grooming lessons and self-serve yourself with a bit of beauty whenever you need a fill up.

*"Think of the magic of that foot upon which your whole weight rests. It's a miracle."*
-Martha Graham

**The Pedals & Peppermint Pedicure**
**Tools Needed:**
**Nail clippers & emery board**
**Foot soak or bath salts**
**A pumice stone**
**Heavy duty foot cream**
**Orangewood stick**
**Nail polish remover**
**Nail Polish**
**Toe separator**
**1 fresh orange (optional)**
**Petals from favorite flower (optional)**

## 4.   Get Soaked

Start by removing old polish and soaking your feet in warm water for at least 10 minutes. A foot bath will both prep your feet by softening skin and it will help relax your over worked muscles.

## 5.   Mint Scrub Smoothie

For feet that are smooth operators, slough off calluses and dry skin with a pumice stone, while your feet are still wet. Next, gently massage feet and ankles with a loofah or exfoliator. I like to use a peppermint foot scrub to ensure all dead skin cells are rubbed off. Rinse your feet and dry thoroughly with a towel.

## 6.   Snip & Shape

Push back cuticles with an orange stick and trim away those that are ragged. When trimming cuticles carefully, use a cuticle cutter which can be found in the beauty section of most grocery or drug stores. Clip nails with toenail clipper straight across and file giving toe nails a square shape and smooth edge with an emery board.

1. **Rubbed the Right Way**

Massage feet with a body oil or heavy lotion for at least five minutes. Choose a scent that you adore.

2. **Polished Presentation**

Remove all oils from toenail surface with polish remover. Apply base coat of clear matte polish, followed by two coats of your favorite color enamel and top off with at least 10 minutes between coats and twenty five minutes once completed.

## Pampering for Quick Feet

If you're really on the go, but you need your soles to survive your travels, here's a quick little foot soak to the rescue. Try it and relax. Your feet will feel fabulous! Grab some Vaseline, a little bit of peppermint essential oil and your favorite sea salts.

## Sole Survivor Foot Scrub

1. Fill your bathtub or another large container with warm water. Allow your skin to soften and your feet to relax as they soak for about 15 minutes.
2. Melt a ¼ cup of Vaseline in a bowl over boiling water. In another bowl, add six drops of essential peppermint oil to ¼ cup of sea salt and stir. Put the mixture into the warm water Vaseline and blend.

3. Use the Vaseline formula and begin to massage your feet. Work especially on the calluses. A pumice stone can be used for additional exfoliation. When you've finished, take a wash cloth and wipe your feet clean. Put on a pair of soft cotton socks to allow the formula to continue to rejuvenate and moisturize your feet.

## The Mellow-Out Manicure

- First soak the nails in warm or very warm sudsy water. Add colorful marbles in the bottom of the bowl and allow your fingers to roll around on them. This helps cleanse underneath the nails and soften the cuticles. It is also very relaxing. Rest quietly as you soak your hands.
- File and round or square off the nail with an emery board. Be sure to file in one direction as to avoid damaging the tips of your nail.
- Use a cuticle stick at the base of the nail. Your nails grow better and look a lot cleaner when you push back the cuticles. Finish by trimming any extra skin or hangnails.
- Massage Vitamin E into the nail base to strengthen you nail and help prevent future hangnails. Rub the oil softly onto the nail and around the edge of the finger.
- Applying a white manicuring pencil underneath the edge of the nail creates a French manicure look without polishing. If you choose, apply the color of your choice.

## Sweet Soothing Facial

Home sweet home is even more delicious when you add a soothing facial to your morning or afternoon delight. This facial includes the three basic elements: Cleansing, toning and masking. Put this facial on your home spa agenda for a relaxing and a calm beauty that radiates inside and out.

## Step 1

Before cleansing your skin with a gentle cleanser, it is advised that you give yourself a light steam treatment to open the pores and set up your face for cleaning. For a light steaming, simply prepare a bowl of comfortably warm herbal tea (orange spice or chamomile work great). Hold your face over a bowl, 5 inches away for about one minute. Next, soak your softest towel in the bowl. Wring out the towel and place it over your face and neck area and relax until it cools slightly. You may repeat this process, if desired.

## Step 2

Cleanse your face with a gentle cleanser. Use upward, circular movements of the fingertips to gently invigorate the skin and help wash away debris and excess oil. Repeat the process until you are sure your face is clean, especially if you wear a lot of makeup. Carefully rinse with warm water and gently pat face with a soft, dry towel.

## Step 3

Apply your toner with a soft cotton pad, by saturating the pad and patting the toner over your face and neck. Allow your skin to air-dry. Avoid eye area when using toner.

## Step 4

Gently apply moisturizer to your face and neck using patting motions. For oily skin, one application is sufficient. Apply twice to dry skin, waiting about 2-3 minutes between applications.

## Shaving How-To's for Ladies

**• Shave Under Water**

Shave during a shower or bath, when hair is wet and your skin is supple. This will cut down on nicks and help you get a close shave. Use a non-soap gel, cream or shaving oil.

**• Always be Sharp and Clean**

Disposable blades are usually the best. Make sure the blade is clean and sharp. Starting with a fresh blade at each shaving will minimize nicks. Razors made for women offer the most comfortable, closest shave.

- **Use a Light Stroke**

    Generally, it's best to move the blade in the opposite direction of the hair growth. Take your time. I usually turn my shaving night into a beauty ritual, with music playing in the bathroom. Pretty colorful razors packed into a clean plastic cup and shaving crème in a fuchsia container with a sweet strawberry aroma, makes the experience pleasurable. Pay close attention to shave spots like ankles, back of knees and thighs.

- **Be Cool**

    Rinse with cool water to close pores. Then lather and use a rub with alcohol free moisturizer to prevent flaking.

- **Avoid Hairy Times Ahead**

    How often should you shave legs and underarms really depends on how fast your hair grows out. I have a schedule to do so every other week.

There's something about taking care of yourself that stirs your creativity and creates a flood of inspiration. Some of my most life-changing ideas have come while I was pampering myself.

## Priceless Pampering

Make it a habit to pay attention to your self completely and carefully. Maintain your body and mind as if you were taking care of a priceless piece of art...because you are. You are a designer original which makes you priceless; now become priceless to your self. Yes, you need to pamper yourself; it is a must. Delicate care of you and your soul gives you the patience, stamina and peace of mind to enjoy life and make life enjoyable for others.

# CREATE A COLLAGE

Designing My Life to Enjoy:

## Pampering

**Use the layout on the following page to design your vision in this area. Get glue sticks, magazines and cut out words and pictures to create an Enjoy Life Collage.**

Wouldn't you love to indulge in a few days of pampering at a lovely spa? What is the pampering experience that you can't live without? Is it a pedicure, manicure or facial? Think of ways to equip yourself for a great home-spa experience. Create a page that illustrates your pampering delights.

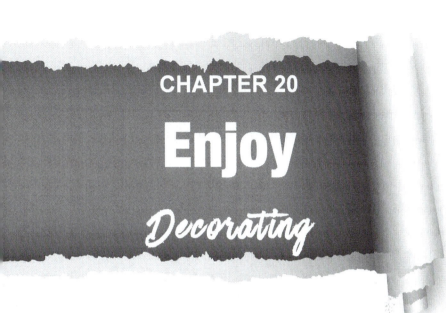

# CHAPTER 20

# Enjoy

## Decorating

*"Houses never truly sing until personal style unfolds."*

*-Charlotte Moss*

The joy in your life begins at home. It is the place where you learn, love and laugh. The home is where the foundation of all your beliefs are laid. It seems a bit simplistic to say that your home is somewhere you should enjoy, but it is essential that you love the interiors in which you dwell. That is why we decorate. However, decorating is not merely placing a flower pot here or hanging a painting there. More so, it is about creating an entire environment.

As we update and stylize our interiors, we must conclude our renovations with more than visual eye candy. Your home must be comfort and pleasure all around. So as you hunt and gather with the ideas and information here, think of how you can make your house a home. Since we've discussed the scent of your home in Chapter 11, let's move on to SIGHT.

# SIGHT

Sight: Designing Insight for Creative Interiors

It's the little things in life that can drive us nuts. Though it may appear to be a small issue, if the surroundings in your home are not visually pleasant to you, it can hinder your ability to think clearly or relax. If the place in which you return each day is unpleasant, the majority of your life will be filled with drudgery. Executing a well-thought out plan to enhance the visual state of your home will do much more than simply please the eye. "Taking steps to enjoy the appearance of your home will help you and your family stay motivated to function properly." Whatever the condition of your home or estate, take "decorating action" to increase the value and "enjoyment potential" of the place in which you live.

The personal style of (you and your spouse if you're married) will dictate the style of your home. Choose colors, furniture, fabrics and objects for your home to be upbeat and filled with colors that are eye catching. I use my home to inspire my giftings. You will not be inspired or even able to think if your house is filled with clutter. Consequently, our first mission must be to clean all clutter, edit your living space and discard the unnecessary. Create order and find a place for everything.

The primary goal of decorating your home should be to create an environment that speaks volumes about who you are and provides the motivation to get you where you are going. To enjoy decorating doesn't have to cost you a fortune, what you spend is totally up to you. My home is a work in progress. I'm always rearranging and updating things. Don't wait for a massive reconstruction project before you begin to add your personal touch to your home. Consistently improve things little by little and each room will eventually become your work of art.

Before you begin a decorating project you must have a vision for the type of atmosphere you want in your home. Answer the following questions and gain insight for your interior decorating.

- **When someone comes into your home, what would you like their assumption to be about you and your family?**
- **What do you want your home to feel like?**

- What are the favorite colors of you and your spouse?
- What are your children's favorite colors?
- Where do your children like to do their homework?
- How much time do you want to spend in each room in the house?
- Do you entertain? How many guests at once?
- Do you work on any projects from home? If so, what are they?
- What do you collect? Would you like it displayed?
- How important is art to you?
- Is your home alive with memories?
- How can you make it more memorable?
- Has your home style grown?
- Do you need to integrate some freshness?

**Color Your Living Space**

Adapt the grandeur of color to suit your comfort needs for today. Color your home with hues that incite emotional support. Do you need to be inspired, comforted or maybe energized? Whatever your needs, use color to fortify your feelings. Be sure that your walls are the perfect backdrop for the furniture and artwork you choose to design your room with. Review the palette below.

**Red:** Attention grabbing red is great for small spaces. As a background color it adds life to the insides of cabinets or armoires and looks especially striking with dark wood. If you have even a hint of red in your flooring or a room with oriental décor, a red wall may be what you need to complete a look that dazzles.

**Orange:** Not only are shades of oranges quite easy to coordinate with other colors, these peachy hues are warm and flattering to the skin. Used in a dining area, shades of orange spark the appetite. Bright shades of orange are playful for children's areas and pleasant notes of orange are a great backdrop for happy times in the family room.

**Yellow:** The brightness of yellow alludes to the sun and is uplifting in rooms without windows. Though it's said that it is a poor choice for an infant's room, it's perfect in rooms for gatherings, entry ways and dining areas.

**Green:** Adds calmness and stability to any room. Blue-Green creates a restful air in the bedroom. Use softer green along with blue-green to create a spa-like atmosphere at home.

**Pink:** Pink can be used by itself to convey a playful and childlike feel to a room. Or it can be paired with stronger colors like black or navy to reflect the beauty and power of a woman. Too much pink in a living and dining room can be a horrifying experience, so tone it down by using darker shades of pink or bits of pink in a lovely pattern.

**Purple:** Royal in its own right. Purple commands attention and adds richness to your décor. It looks great in the kitchen. Tones of grapes, lilac and lavender are sophisticated and create a lovely ambiance in the bathroom, dining and living room. Being reminiscent of luscious fruits, deep shades of purple also look great in the kitchen.

**White:** Giving your home a backdrop in tones of creamy white provides you with a clear canvas on which to let your creativity run wild. Remember that pure white is very bright. So if you are looking for serenity, a soft shade of off-white will do.

### Bright is Alright

Don't be afraid to incorporate bright colors into you décor. Decide on a color scheme and execute a well thought out plan. When used correctly color provides a visual shock that is invigorating and enlightening for your home interiors.

### What's your Scheme?

Put your stamp of approval on your home by choosing a color scheme filled with hues that you love.

First, begin reviewing a number of colors that you like. A color wheel is helpful in this endeavor. A traditional color wheel is made up of colors arranged in a circle with primary colors at one-third intervals. Check your local art store or with an interior designer to get one you can look at. You can create your personal version of a color wheel by collecting paper in bright colors that you like. By punching a hole in the corner of each sheet and connecting the sheets with a metal ring. This will allow you to flip through your colors with ease while making your decorating choices.

When working on your color scheme, try to choose colors that complement each other. Colors that are opposite of each other on the color wheel are complementary. For example, red and green or purple and yellow are complements. When choosing bright complements, be sure to evaluate how long your personal style can really live with these colors. I love bright colors in my living spaces. However, if I am leery of my tolerance level for a certain color, I accent the room with that color and use a shade of white as the backdrop. Shocking combinations may best be used in a kitchen, children's room or creative art space. In your bedroom, such combinations may prove to be exhausting. Play around with fabric swatches and colored paper to get an idea of the colors you love to group together.

**Living in the Light**

When decorating a room consider how you plan to use lighting to add the final touches. Your lighting choices can invade or accessorize a room.

After designating a purpose for the place in your home, use the lighting that is consistent with that purpose. If the space is a study area, lights should be bright and refreshing, making it an easy place to read.

In the dining area or rooms in which you entertain, it is convenient to have lights with a dimmer or other types of adjustment knobs. This gives you the flexibility to switch your light settings based on the nature of your event. For example, use bright lights for pre ballet hors d'ouvres or dimmed lights for an intimate dinner.

Allowing natural light to flow throughout our home makes for healthier, happier living. Open windows, patio doors and shades when the weather is agreeable. Whatever you do, don't keep your house closed up as if it were abandoned. Be mindful that while sunlight is necessary for happy humans, it also had the power to ruin items in your rooms. Painting, drawings, photographs and even fine wood all deteriorate when exposed to excessive sunlight.

Turn to the light as an additional tool to set the mood in your home. The proper lighting within your interiors is not only a sound investment, but a must. Collaborate by using natural and electrical light to increase your efficiency and promote your overall feeling of well-being.

## Collecting

What you collect says a lot about who you are. Decorating around things you collect adds an exclusive ambience to your home. My kitchen walls are lined with beautiful, motivational quotes & paintings. I strongly believe that what you focus on and say becomes real in your life. So when I decided to redecorate this space, I thought about how the kitchen's the hub of our house and we spend the majority of our time there. So what better way to add some positive thoughts and conversation to my family's days, than with a gallery of quotes.

Gathering and displaying your finds is a fun way to decorate. It adds individuality to your home. What special things do you or your mate collect? If you don't collect anything yet, then keep your eyes open for items that might inspire you. Remember that the most substantial reason to collect anything is because it's appealing to you. The items may spark a memory from your past or be a significant piece of history. Whatever the case, it is purely for your enjoyment. I'm very passionate about everything that I collect; like boxes, tea cups, paper and fashion table books. As you take in items that you are passionate about, you will develop stunning collections just as I have.

### Children's Collections

When building a children's collection the focus is to gather fascinating items that in some way stir up their creative side. The objects become a catalyst for conversation and self-discovery. What a child collects may have something to do with his or her future purpose in life. My daughter has always loved to collect journals. To this day, every time we see one that stands out to her, she gets it. In your decorating process for you and your children, find neat places to hold your valuable pieces.

*"Go on decorating field trips."*

*-Dr. Stacia Pierce*

### See the Future

Start clipping and filing away designs that appeal to you before you make any purchases to decorate your house. Get your self about three to four home magazines and pull out pictures of rooms, appliances and paint colors that appeal to you. I created a collage of my home design in my *Millionaire's Dream Book* pages with styles I really loved from magazine clippings. After you've placed your pictures, write on them what in particular you like about them, so when you go back to look at a later date, you will know why you chose that photo.

# TOUCH

## Pillow Talk

Decorating your bedroom is a very important task. Your bed itself is the most utilized piece of furniture in the home. The right bed will keep you well rested and energized. When we were searching for our new bed, I knew that all of the components had to be in place. The bed needed a sturdy backboard, because both my husband and I frequently read and write in bed for hours at a time. Most of us spend an average of 12 hours in our bedrooms. To meet our needs, femininity and masculinity had to coincide within the design of the bed. Researchers have said the bed is where you will spend roughly 220,000 hours of your life. Inadequate sleep can lead to stress, a short temper, low motivation, irritability, mistakes and slow reflexes. The way you sleep every night determines how you feel every day. A good mattress is an essential ingredient when decorating. You can determine whether or not you need a new mattress by the quality of your sleep.

### Bed Linens

I've grown up loving bed linens. Matching beautiful sheets and comforters were an essential part of my household as a young girl. Upgrading your bed linens is one of the easiest and fastest ways to decorate your bedroom. But making a proper choice is important. The fiber type and quality play a part in how comfortable the linen will be. The buzzword of the bedding industry is thread count, which is the number of threads in one square inch of fabric. It may seem menial, but it is significant when considering a fabric's elasticity and durability. Usually, a higher thread count, plus the quality of the fiber, equals a long-lasting, comfortable set of sheets.

A thread count of 350 or more results in the softest and most durable sheets. You'll save money when you buy higher quality sheets because you won't have to replace them as frequently. The next time you are shopping for sheets, purchase the highest thread count you can afford.

You can add your signature style to your bed linens and even bathroom towels by having them monogrammed. Stately initials or names on linens add a touch of class and flair.

The main thing to remember is to choose colors and patterns for linens, which reflect your personal style. Your bedroom should be very inviting, especially since you must spend so much time there. Why not spruce up your intimate apparel collection as well? I only wear pajamas that I love in every aspect: the fit, color, fabric, etc. Get some outfits that match the colors of your bedroom. It's nice to also have lounge wear. Keep a few elaborate pieces in your collection for evenings when you dine with your spouse.

## HOW TO CARE FOR BED LINENS

- Wash new sheets in warm water and tumble dry on medium heat before using.

- Add flare to your linen set by arranging sheets by color or tying them in a pretty ribbon until it's time to use them.

- To brighten white sheets: add ¼ cup of lemon juice to wash cycle. If possible, line dry in the sun.

- Fold sheets while still warm to minimize wrinkling.

## HOW TO GET A GOOD NIGHT'S SLEEP

1. Stick to a regular schedule for going to bed and getting up.
2. Unwind before going to bed, believe it or not I usually exercise in the evening then take a long, hot pampering shower about 2-3 hours before I go to bed.
3. Develop a bedtime routine. It will signal your body when it's time to settle down. My bedtime routine consists of washing my face, brushing my teeth and usually reading.
4. Avoid going to bed too full or hungry. Either condition makes way for a restless night's slumber.

### Getting Inspired

One of my primary sources for gathering information is home magazines. Home decorating books will also educate you on decorating as well as offer ideas.

Keep a journal handy and write down the details of anything that catches your eye and the pricing information. It is very easy to forget where you saw "the piece that would fit perfectly with your kitchen" when trying to recall it later. Absorb life, keep your eyes open and get inspiration from everything around you. Put as many details as possible in your journal about how you want your current home and your dream designed.

### Creating a Home Design Board

Start compiling snippets of fabrics, ribbons, paint swatches and trimmings. Keep gift-wrapping paper or even product packaging that jumps out at you. Divide your design board up into room headings and tack everything that you are considering for that room under that category. This will give you the opportunity to test the look and feel of that room with your color and fabric before you actually spend the money to redesign it.

### Be Conscious of Their Feelings

Whether you have a full house or live alone, go through your home and find out where you can make improvements to the items that touch your household each day.

### Showerheads

Maybe you need a new showerhead that adjusts to different pressures so the water feels just right when it hits your skin.

### Under Your Feet

Keep your carpet soft and fresh by having it professionally cleaned periodically. Sweep them off their feet by practicing extreme cleanliness when it comes to hardwood floors. Yucky is the word that comes to mind when I think of walking barefoot on a crumb-infested floor.

### What's in your Wash?

Use special fabric softeners in loads of laundry for soft fluffy towels and fresh smelling clothes you love to slip into.

### Sitting Pretty

Consider the fabric texture when purchasing new furniture. Put a soft blanket in the family living area. In case some one in your home needs a little extra coziness.

# SOUND

The gentle drops of rain, the voices of people we love, the busyness of downtown rush hour or the symphony of nature on a summer morning are all a part of the sounds of life. Hearing is a powerful thing. It enables you to digest and understand your surroundings. Sharing the right things builds your faith, increases our motivation and knowledge and instills confidence. Hearing the wrong things invites fear, numbs our thought process and destroys our self-image. What sounds are being played over with noise or generally serene; strive for "home" peace when working on your interiors.

### Fresh Air

Don't let your home have an argumentative air. As much as possible speak respectfully to those in your household to keep bitterness and tension out of the atmosphere.

### Play Inspirational Music

Music has the ability to affect both our behavior and attitude. Certain classical pieces are great for studying. Dance music is great to clean your house or workout to.

### Play Inspirational Audio Messages or Books

For at least an hour a day I play a motivational message or audiobook to increase my knowledge and keep me motivated. You can download your favorite files to your phone or tablet.

# TASTE

A person's first taste of life comes from their household. Make sure that you leave those in your home with tasty memories of the wonderful things in your household. Leave inviting bowls of fresh fruit on the counters. Create meal plans to ensure that you and your household are eating healthy meals. Even if you hire a cook to prepare them. If you are a mother, be sure that before your children are grown that they have some recollection of yummy home styled meals. On occasion, your family's mouths should water for something you cook. Whatever your specialty, take the time to serve your family something you lovingly prepared for them. That is all a part of enjoyable living.

# Designing Don'ts

- Don't over collect small objects. Too many small things clutter a room and look messy.

- Don't separate your collections and place them all around the house. Instead, for esthetic purposes, keep them all together displayed in one place.

- Don't be afraid to use color. Vivid colors can add a remarkable bit of chic to your home. Even if it's just a painting or a single wall in a shade you love.

- Don't put a bunch of small items in a small room. Even a small room can use an over-scaled item to make a statement.

- Don't decorate without a plan. Let your magazine tear sheets be your guide, but be sure to pare down to one consistent look you are going for.

- Don't forget about your male counterparts when decorating, men like things comfortable, not dainty.

- Don't forget to upgrade little things that can make a huge difference, like lampshades, valances, curtains and blinds.

- Don't forget to unclutter every room in your house. Less is more.

# CREATE a COLLAGE

Designing My Life to Enjoy:

## Decorating

**Use the layout on the following page to design your vision in this area. Get glue sticks, magazines and cut out words and pictures to create an Enjoy Life Collage.**

What does your dream home look like? In what ways would you like your home to be inviting to all of your senses? Find bright sheets of paper in your favorite colors. Create a page that shows how you imagine your interior.

Designing a Life to Enjoy

# CREATE A COLLAGE
LifeCoach2Women.com

# CHAPTER 21

# Enjoy

## Personal Space

*"My idea of a home is a house which each member of the family can on the instant, kindle a fire, in his or her private room."*
**-Ralph Waldo Emerson**

No matter where she lives or what she does, every woman needs a place to get away. It's much easier to live an enjoyable life when you have a zone of retreat. Every woman needs a personal space, a private place she can call her own. To be a woman today means functioning in multiple roles, seeing to various interests and nurturing those around you. Due to these responsibilities, you must have a location to restore your spirit. We cannot enjoy the freedoms of achieving goals, loving relationships and fulfilling purpose if we do not have private getaways. Without a personal space you will tend to feel neglected, cheated and unnerved. Whenever we shut out the world and all of its demands, we can reflect on what's brought us this far and imagine how we can go further. Give yourself gifts of time in your personal space, so you can develop the stamina, balance and wisdom to master the art of living.

Since the beginning of time great women have used their private quarters as thinking tanks; the places where their outstanding contributions to society began. The work world be void of their pioneering accomplishments had these women not made use of their personal space.

### Madame C. J. Walker

Madame Walker was the first woman entrepreneur to become a millionaire. She gained her fortune through the beauty industry selling hair care products for African American women; which was no small feat for a black woman during the early nineteen hundreds. She developed her first hair care products in her favorite spot, the kitchen. After she became rich, she had a special room built upstairs in her elegantly designed mansion. Madame Walker had the room decorated with comfortable furniture, beautiful window coverings, fresh flowers and her favorite Bible. She said that the room was built to give her a place to sit alone quietly to think, read, and pray.

### Eleanor Ford

The wife of Edsel Ford ran their vast estate and mapped out the lifestyle of her elite family from her "planning room." In this room, on the upper level of the estate, was a beautiful desk where she spent the early hours of the day, unknowingly making history. During my visit to the estate, I was in awe to see the way the Ford home was cared for. The instructions Eleanor gave from her personal space were still meticulously followed long after her death.

### Barbara McClintock

Barbara was recognized with a Nobel Prize for medicine in 1983. She was awarded for genetic research that she had done some forty years earlier. Considered a genius, her two-bedroom getaway on top of the garage was where she did 50 years of research. Today the scientific community names her among the three top geneticists in history. Happy and content to work hours in her lab over the garage, Barbara demonstrates that a personal space and a merry heart does good like a medicine.

## Helen Keller

Spending many hours in the parlor of her home, Helen Keller gained victory over seemingly insurmountable disabilities. Keller became deaf and blind as a result of a severe case of scarlet fever during childhood. Nevertheless, Helen Keller is one of the most well known advocates for women's suffrage and the rights of the physically disabled. Those precious moments studying and developing in the parlor both alone and with her teacher, Anne Sullivan, became the foundation of her success.

## Mary Quant

A pioneer in the women's fashion industry in the 60's, Mary Quant popularized the miniskirt and patterned belle bottoms. Many stars shopped in her London boutique, but it was her marketing techniques that made her a household name. Where did she sketch her fabulous designs and develop her ingenious marketing plans? In the corner of her living room, within her stylish London flat, Mary designed the unforgettable on a large wooden table stocked with all her art supplies. Making use of just a little personal space, Mrs. Quant revolutionized the fashion industry. Dare to dream from your personal space, even if it's only a tabletop.

What are the most inspiring places for you? My home is it at the top of my list. Next would have to be bookstores. Lastly, I've decorated my office so that it also provides a creative lift. Go to those places of inspiration and draw from them, but don't neglect to set aside a space in your home. Make space for you to focus. Neglecting to stop and examine your life is a guarantee that you will lose focus on your assignment or worse yet never discover it at all. Your own personal space is the location where you are reminded that you have a purpose and there is a unique plan for your life that must be fulfilled.

By now I'm sure you have begun to take note of how a personal space can benefit you.

 **It's a place where you can slow down and reflect.**

 **A place where you can have moments of silence.**

 **It serves as a creative think spot.**

**It's a place to meditate.**

 **It's a place to plan your day.**

 **You can use it to display a collection of things that are meaningful**

 **It's a place to work on a hobby, which could be a connection to your purpose.**

### Space Finding

Designing your private camp could be as simple as setting up a chair and an end table with fresh flowers on top. You could also turn an abandoned closet into a "wrapping center". Find the space you want then load it with tools that spark your creativity and enable you to work on special projects. Use the corner of your kitchen and bring in a desk and lamp that match the colors of the décor and fit your personal style.

A small space in your living room could turn into your private oasis. Some ladies use beautiful screens to create a space within a room. In one of my homes I turned a corner of my formal living room into a mini library by adding contemporary portable shelves. Now my extensive book collection is stylishly displayed and offers me an intriguing place to sit and learn. Whatever space you have available, utilize it.

Your bedroom could be your sanctuary. If you are married, realize that you must consider your husband's needs in the room as well. Your husband may not appreciate your décor if the entire bedroom is oozing with "Pepto Bismal Pink", floral prints and lace. Find out what colors and designs appeal to him and figure out a way to include his tastes in the décor.

You do not have to seize the entire room. You may want to designate a dressing table as your private spot or take over a corner of the room. I have captured the corner next to my side of the bed. I journalize and read in my bed quite a bit. When everything is quiet and you have a minute to rest, you can turn your private space into your very own sanctuary.

I love to read, write, journalize and listen to audios in my bedroom, so I decorated it with cheerful colors and things that I love. My nightstand holds a colorful array of my writing utensils. Highlighters, gel pens and shocking pink sticky notepads fill a deep fuchsia container next to my lamp. With such delightful instruments to write with, it's fun to journalize. Due to the convenience of having all the utensils I need right at my fingertips, relaxing and getting right down to business is easy. Everything I can think of is within arms length and most importantly, I don't have to waste my time searching the house for a pen or a highlighter.

If you have a sunroom, that is a wonderful place to claim as your special spot. Unlike my room which is ideal for personal reflection, the library is more for my creative thinking. I like to plan for special events and parties, have meetings, do tea alone and write letters in this room. The room is so upbeat and cheery that it's a great place to jot down an encouraging note to a friend.

### Personal Spaces R Us

Our home is set up so that each of us have a personal space. In these places we can house all the tech toys, books and journals that we love. Creating a space that can be enjoyed for hours of personal time is important. Designing in an inspiring place created just for them, I decorated my children's rooms with love. As they've become  young adults, their passions have grown and their interests become my inspiration to create the perfect environment for them to relax and begin their days. I always wanted their rooms to be enjoyed by their guests as well. Changes are continually made as our tastes or seasons change. Yet, one thing is consistent; every rooms changes to express what's most important to them at the time.

If you have children, investigate and find out what they really love. Is it a favorite character, if they are younger? What are their favorite colors? Discover their hobbies and passions. Should you put a drafting table in their room? A personal computer stationed at a comfortable desk will assist them in their quest to learn. Of course, in the day in which we live, computer time and phone use must be heavily monitored by you as the parent for safety and appropriate exposure for your children.

Allow your children (ages 3-18), to have some part in the decorating process. Find out what's important to them and incorporate their input into your plans. Equipping your children with a personal space that is arranged to flow with their natural gifting and preferences, will help them stay on the course of destiny.

For you married ladies, help your husband find a spot he can call his own. My husband has an entertainment room in our home. This is where he has his large screen TV and media cabinet with all his favorite movies, games and etc. He and my son Ryan have lots of fun and spend special time together in this space. My husband also has a space where he studies and prepares his messages that inspires and sparks creativity for him. Every member of your household needs to feel like they have a place to think and ponder, a place for them to escape and enjoy their home.

## How to Use Your Personal Space

### 1. Use it as Place to Meditate
Meditate on your dreams and goals.

### 2. Use it to Fulfill Your Purpose
Prepare for purpose in your private quarters. Listen to or read about great motivational speakers or coaches.

### 3.  Use it as a Creativity Storehouse
Stock your personal space with materials that spark interest.


### 4.  Use it as a Future Statement
Name your personal space with a title that describes who you are and what you do.


### 5.  Use it to Display Your Collections
Fill it with things that you love.


### 6.  Use it to Plan your Day
Whether early in the morning or late at night before you retire, write out your to-do list in your personal space.


### 7.  Use it to take Time Out
Relax. This is your time.


My personal space serves me well. It's where I continue to evolve. Determine that your life will be marked by greatness. You have something to offer the world. Develop it. Mark the spot where you will prepare. Stake claim to a room, desktop corner or chair. Whatever it is you choose, designate a space in your home to reflect your style, gain clarity of direction and restore your ability to dream.

# CREATE a COLLAGE

Designing My Life to Enjoy:

## Personal Space

**Use the layout on the following page to design your vision in this area. Get glue sticks, magazines and cut out words and pictures to create an Enjoy Life Collage.**

Imagine the ideal spot for your personal space. What does it look like? What tools or pieces of furniture does it include? Sit for a moment and decide what you will name your space. Create a page that illustrates who you are and what you do and the personal space in which you make it happen.

Designing a Life to Enjoy

# CREATE A COLLAGE
LifeCoach2Women.com

## ABOUT THE AUTHOR

**Award-Winning Life Coach, Motivational Speaker & Entrepreneur**

When you first get a glimpse of what a single day in the life of Stacia Pierce entails, you begin to wonder if she somehow has more than 24 hours in her day. Your first encounter with this award-winning Life Coach is guaranteed to be a whirlwind of passion, excitement and motivation bundled up into a highly-acclaimed business woman, paving the way for the limitless success of her clients.

With a contagious energy and an impressive roster of motivational and entrepreneurial successes, Ultimate Lifestyle Enterprises Founder and CEO, Stacia Pierce has taken empowerment to an entirely new level by helping others turn obstacles into opportunities.

A living example of success, Pierce was named Top Women Who Mean Business by the Orlando Business Journal for her system of turning passions into paychecks, enabling her to motivate fellow entrepreneurs worldwide. Pierce has worked with everyone from the Hollywood elite, to Grammy- and Emmy-winners, to television personalities, several successful business owners, lawyers, doctors and government officials throughout the United States, Canada, and the Bahamas.

Her 'No Excuses' business philosophy encourages clients to take responsibility for every aspect of their lives and businesses. Pierce has also developed her highly-acclaimed 'Success Attractions Strategies', a vast collection of success tools, seminars and conferences triggering exploration of self-creativity, while embracing the possibilities of a better, more fulfilling and healthier way of life.

And it doesn't stop there! Pierce also created several additional success tools to encourage the adaptation of reaching your highest potential. Dubbed a 'Whole Life Coach', she has mastered the art of overhauling the lives of clients, leading them to discover their true selves, as well as their true potential.

With the use of straight-to-the-point, candid stories and highly-charged anecdotes, she inspires people to find their inner 'Dream Driver'. Regardless of the goal, Pierce focuses her unwavering dedication to empower women to freely and smartly chase their greatest desires with confidence and knowledge.

Her educational successes are equally impressive having earned a Doctorate of Philosophy and Religious Studies from Friends International University, as well as a Doctorate of Divinity from St. Thomas College. Outstanding community service projects like the Women Caring for Women event, and the entrepreneur economic improvement program's, Shop and Swap Professional Empowerment event, have earned her additional honors.

With books, newsletters, retail products, appearances and countless online outlets as part of her growing empire, Pierce is able to inspire over 100,000 people weekly.

She is a native of Grand Rapids, Michigan and currently resides in Central Florida, with her husband, Dr. James and their two children, Ariana and Ryan.

**Contact Dr. Stacia at**
**stacia@lifecoach2women.com**

*******

## BOOKS BY DR. STACIA

**You can order these books and other products by Dr. Stacia by logging onto** www.lifecoach2women.com

Success Attraction Notes & Quotes

The Success Secrets of a Reader

My Life in Style

The Success Journal

*******

\*\*\*\*\*\*\*

## *MEDIA RESOURCES*

**At last!  Websites to empower your dreams and make success your reality.**

www.lifecoach2women.com
**Main website & event information**

www.youtube.com/lifecoach2women
**Events and biography video**

\*\*\*\*\*\*\*

@DrStaciaPierce   @StaciaPierce   @LifeCoach2Women

@LifeCoach2Women        @StaciaPierce

LifeCoach2Women.com

## TODAY'S DREAMS DETERMINE YOUR TOMORROW! The Millionaire's Dream Book

Anyone who has achieved success started with a vision to do and become more. *The Millionaire's Dream Book* is an easy to use system from Dr. Stacia Pierce which utilizes the power of pictures and words to help you see your way to success.

This is the road map your dream you've been waiting for. This incredible tool helps you catalog your dreams, and stay focused on your future as you head in the direction of your future success. You will be empowered to:

\* Visualize better ideas and strategies for your success

* Chart your progress and stay encouraged to succeed

* Plan with pictures to accelerate the execution of your goals


Go beyond your reality and envision new realms of possibility with Stacia's *Millionaire's Dream Book*. Now is the time to do something about your dreams. If you've ever wanted to see beyond today and success in the future, The Millionaire's Dream Book is for you. Invest now, get yours and begin framing your future. Before you know it you'll flow with ideas that will help you bring your pages to life!

**Order Now at** www.lifecoach2women.com!